Dying for a Drink

Dr Tim Cantopher studied at University College, London and University College Hospital. He trained as a psychiatrist at St James' Hospital, Portsmouth and St George's Hospital Medical School. He has been a member of the Royal College of Psychiatrists since 1983 and was elected fellow of the college in 1999. He is now a Consultant Psychiatrist working with the Priory Group of Hospitals. This is Dr Cantopher's third book, and he has published a number of research projects across the field of psychiatry. Dr Cantopher is married with three children and lives in Surrey. He is the author of *Depressive Illness: The curse of the strong* (Sheldon, 2003, 2006) and *Stress-related Illness* (Sheldon, 2007).

Overcoming Common Problems Series

Selected titles

A full list of titles is available from Sheldon Press,
36 Causton Street, London SW1P 4ST and on our website at
www.sheldonpress.co.uk

101 Questions to Ask Your Doctor
Dr Tom Smith

Asperger Syndrome in Adults
Dr Ruth Searle

Bulimia, Binge-eating and their Treatment
Professor J. Hubert Lacey, Dr Bryony Bamford
and Amy Brown

Coeliac Disease: What you need to know
Alex Gazzola

Coping Successfully with Prostate Cancer
Dr Tom Smith

Coping When Your Child Has Cerebral Palsy
Jill Eckersley

Coping with Bronchitis and Emphysema
Dr Tom Smith

Coping with Chemotherapy
Dr Terry Priestman

Coping with Dyspraxia
Jill Eckersley

Coping with Early-onset Dementia
Jill Eckersley

Coping with Envy
Dr Windy Dryden

Coping with Gout
Christine Craggs-Hinton

**Coping with Life's Challenges: Moving on
from adversity**
Dr Windy Dryden

Coping with Phobias and Panic
Professor Kevin Gournay

**Coping with the Psychological Effects
of Cancer**
Professor Robert Bor, Dr Carina Eriksen
and Ceilidh Stapelkamp

Coping with Rheumatism and Arthritis
Dr Keith Souter

Coping with Snoring and Sleep Apnoea
Jill Eckersley

Coping with Type 2 Diabetes
Susan Elliot-Wright

**Divorce and Separation: A legal guide
for all couples**
Dr Mary Welstead

**Dynamic Breathing: How to manage
your asthma**
Dinah Bradley and Tania Clifton-Smith

**High-risk Body Size: Take control
of your weight**
Dr Funké Baffour

How to Beat Worry and Stress
Dr David Delvin

How to Develop Inner Strength
Dr Windy Dryden

How to Live with a Control Freak
Barbara Baker

**How to Lower Your Blood Pressure:
And keep it down**
Christine Craggs-Hinton

How to Manage Chronic Fatigue
Christine Craggs-Hinton

Hysterectomy: Is it right for you?
Janet Wright

Living with Fibromyalgia
Christine Craggs-Hinton

**Living with a Problem Drinker:
Your survival guide**
Rolande Anderson

Living with a Stoma
Professor Craig A. White

Living with Tinnitus and Hyperacusis
Dr Laurence McKenna, Dr David Baguley
and Dr Don McFerran

Losing a Parent
Fiona Marshall

Menopause in Perspective
Philippa Pigache

Motor Neurone Disease: A family affair
Dr David Oliver

Natural Treatments for Arthritis
Christine Craggs-Hinton

**Overcoming Gambling: A guide for problem
and compulsive gamblers**
Philip Mawer

Sinusitis: Steps to healing
Dr Paul Carson

**Therapy for Beginners: How to get the best
out of counselling**
Professor Robert Bor, Sheila Gill and Anne Stokes

Understanding Traumatic Stress
Dr Nigel Hunt and Dr Sue McHale

When Someone You Love Has Dementia
Susan Elliot-Wright

Overcoming Common Problems

Dying for a Drink

DR TIM CANTOPHER

sheldon PRESS

To Laura

Sheldon Press
36 Causton Street
London SW1P 4ST
www.sheldonpress.co.uk

First published 1996
Second edition 2002

This edition copyright © Tim Cantopher 2011
Cartoons © Sophie Dean

The author and publisher have made every effort to ensure that the external website and email addresses included in this book are correct and up to date at the time of going to press. The author and publisher are not responsible for the content, quality or continuing accessibility of the sites.

British Library Cataloguing-in-Publication Data

A catalogue record for this book is available from the British Library

ISBN 978–1–84709–176–5
eBook ISBN 978–1–84709–177–2

Typeset by Fakenham Prepress Solutions, Fakenham, Norfolk NR21 8NN
First printed in Great Britain by Ashford Colour Press
Subsequently digitally printed in Great Britain

Produced on paper from sustainable forests

Contents

Acknowledgements

I would like to thank all the patients, colleagues and friends who have helped so greatly in the preparation of this book. In particular, I am indebted to the following:

Mrs Jean Hardy and Mrs Trudy Thurston-Moon, for secretarial support with the first edition.

Drs Peter Finch, David Barnes and Paola Franciosi, Mr Neil Springham and particularly the excellent Ms Polly Mair for providing their expertise and preventing me from publishing mistakes that would have shown up embarrassing areas of ignorance.

Thanks also to The Book Guild for originally publishing this book, and to Sheldon Press for their continued faith in me, represented on this occasion by publishing this third edition.

Introduction

'Well, do you drink, doctor?'

The question made me feel a little defensive. It is an old maxim that an alcoholic is someone who drinks more than his doctor. In this case I wasn't at all sure that he did. My questioner, John, had lost his marriage, his job and his driving licence through drinking, but in total his consumption was not that unusual.

'Yes, I do. Around 20 units a week.'

'Oh, yeah? Make that 40 at least.'

The group that I was supposed to be leading collapsed into helpless giggles at the thought of their consultant falling into a drunken stupor behind closed doors. Everyone in the room knew of the phenomenon of underestimating your drinking in your own mind.

As it happens, the keeping of a drink diary has reassured me that my original estimate was accurate, though John was right to recognize that anyone can develop a drink problem. But surely that doesn't apply to you? These people are alcoholics; they all have long histories of harming themselves through their drinking. You only drink to be sociable and join in the party. But hang on, parties don't happen that often and do you really need a drug to cope with social intercourse? Well, maybe you just have a drink at the end of the day to help you relax, because your job is very busy and your lifestyle is very stressed. You get a bit tense; anyone would.

'Same here, doc,' says John. 'That's how I started. Trouble is, now I'm even more tense. Booze does that, you know. Starts off giving you a lift and helping you unwind, but before you know it you're drinking every day, feeling terrible and having a drink to get you going. I'd be a bit careful if I were you, doc. You should cut down.'

More group mirth. I say nothing, keeping a stony professional silence, but my thoughts speak volumes. For goodness sake, I'm supposed to be running this session. If there's one thing that gets up my nose it's a clever Dick. When's this blasted session over anyway? I could do with a drink. Oh dear.

John has succeeded in diverting attention from his own problems. He's good at that. Last week he did it by pointing out that Simon drinks ten times as much as him, and anyway he drinks less than most of his friends. 'If I've got a drink problem, then so has most of the population of Surrey.'

Through his skills at denial, John raises points that concern us all. What or who is an alcoholic? Is an alcoholic born that way? If so, can the rest of us drink happily in the knowledge that it will never happen to us?

My answer to the first question is rather non-specific. To me, an alcoholic is someone who continues to drink when everyone around him knows he should stop.

To the second and third questions I can only reply with a question. (Yes, I know, psychiatrists always do that.) Who has the greater problem, someone who lives on his own, has no dependants and few responsibilities and drinks a bottle of Scotch a day on his own at home, or someone who drinks only once a week, five pints of beer on a Friday evening in the pub with friends from work on the way home from the office? One further piece of information before you decide. Our latter drinker, a man of otherwise impeccable character and habits, drives home after his end-of-week tipple. One Friday evening he knocks over and kills a small child on the way home.

I know who I think has the greater problem, and he looks very like you and me. I think anyone can develop a drink problem; you just have to drink enough for long enough or at the wrong time. To divide the world into 'alcoholics' and 'the rest of us' seems to me to be a denial of our capacity to fall into this trap without even noticing it is happening.

What follows in this book is a few facts and theories about alcohol and drinking gleaned from the people I have worked with – patients, staff, academics, friends and others – as well as something about what to do if you have developed a problem or want to avoid developing one. Hopefully this will be of interest to everyone, because the ways to prevent or overcome a drink problem are also the ways to be happy and healthy. Whether you consider that you or someone close to you has a drink problem or not, I hope that you will find it food for thought – just as John made me think, blast him.

Throughout this book collective terms will be masculine when not referring to a specific gender. I have done this for ease and brevity of expression and it does not denote sex differences unless specified. Examples are given referring to one sex or the other to enable a real person to be visualized, but the gender of the examples was chosen at random and does not imply that the issues described are specific to or more predominant in either sex.

Note: This is not a medical book and is not intended to replace advice from your doctor. Do consult your doctor if you are experiencing symptoms with which you feel you need help.

Part 1
ALCOHOL THE DRUG

1

About alcohol

Alcohol is a drug. Like all drugs, it is dangerous if used in excess. Contrary to widely held belief, it is not desperately addictive, compared, say, to a drug like heroin. The vast majority of people who use heroin become addicted to it. That is, they need to continue taking it to stave off withdrawal symptoms and craving, and they will usually escalate their dose over time. In contrast, only a small proportion of people who use alcohol become addicted to it. About 90 per cent of the population use alcohol at least occasionally, and most keep their usage remarkably constant. Some do not and they will be discussed later.

Despite this, alcohol is really quite a nasty drug. Can you imagine a pharmaceutical firm trying to bring it on to the market as a new drug today? I can imagine the reaction of the Committee on Safety of Medicines, the main regulatory body for drugs in this country.

'So what does this new drug of yours do then?'

'Well, it gives you a lift, makes you feel nice and relaxes you.'

'Hmm. How long does this effect last?'

'Only a few hours, I'm afraid. Over a period of time, in fact, it makes you depressed, anxious and unwell.'

'Oh dear. Does it have any other side effects?'

'Well yes, it does, actually. Hundreds. If used to excess it can cause your liver to fail, give you ulcers, stop the nervous system working properly and lead to brain damage. That's just the start, shall I go on?'

'No, get out and take your lousy drug with you. You're wasting our time. We wouldn't pass that in a million years.'

So why is alcohol so widely used? There are several answers to this. First, it's easy and cheap to make. All you need is a source of sugar, some yeast and water. Second, it has been used for thousands of years.

The word 'alcohol' comes from the Arabic, meaning literally 'all things very fine'. Though Islamic societies are not allowed to drink alcohol, their physicians until relatively recently regarded it as a panacea for all ills. They were not the only ones. Throughout time there has been a strong tradition of the use of alcohol as a medicine, and positive references to its beneficial effects crop up throughout history, from the writings of Hippocrates in ancient Greece and the Old

Testament at the one extreme to textbooks of pharmacology published as recently as the 1940s. The first edition of Goodman and Gilman's standard textbook *The Pharmacological Basis of Therapeutics* describes whisky and champagne as 'the only foods tolerated by febrile and restless patients' and whisky and soda as 'the drink of choice for chronic patients with coronary artery disease'.

The third and probably most important reason why alcohol is still used is political. A lot of people, including politicians, drink it. To prohibit it would be economically catastrophic (though the economic damage done to industry through the harmful effects of alcohol on the health of the workforce is massive). Prohibition, anyway, was tried in the USA and failed.

When we drink alcohol we are to an extent playing with fire, but of course the great majority of people drink quite safely all their lives. It depends largely on how much you drink. In recent years the units system has been introduced, which allows us to get a fair indication of how much we are drinking and whether or not this is safe. Table 1.1 indicates the units of alcohol in many of our commonly consumed drinks. Remember that a home-poured measure is probably more than a pub double.

The guidelines are: for men, it is reasonably safe to drink 21[1] units of alcohol a week or less; and for women, 14 units a week or less. This is not sexism; women metabolize alcohol differently from men: a lower proportion of their bodies is comprised of water, and they are at greater

Table 1.1 Alcohol units in drinks

Single pub measure of spirits (25ml)	1 unit
Home-poured measure of spirits (50–125ml)	2–5 units
Pint of keg beer (3.6%)	2 units
Pint of real ale (5–6%)	3–4 units
Pint of lager (4–6%)	2–4 units
Can of 'special brew' or 'extra' lager (6–8%)	3–4 units
Small schooner of sherry	1 unit
Glass of wine*	1–2 units
Bottle of wine	8–9 units
Bottle of spirits	28–30 units
Litre bottle of 'vintage' cider (8%)	10–12 units

* Normal size (I have wine glasses that hold a pint!)

---

[1]   The government has recently increased this figure to 28 units a week; this is not based on new statistics, but on an acceptance of a slightly higher point on the graph as being 'safe'.

risk of physical and mental complications from an equivalent amount of alcohol. It doesn't mean that men are safe; far from it. Between 22 and 50 units weekly for men and between 15 and 35 units for women puts you in the intermediate risk category, while if you drink over 50 units weekly (men) or 35 units weekly (women), you are at high risk.

But who decides on these figures? They sound arbitrary and one tends to suspect that they have been dreamt up by some official in Brussels to annoy us and interfere with our lives, like litres, kilograms and ECUs. In fact, this isn't the case, as you will see from Figure 1.1.

Your risk of death rises with the amount that you drink. There is an idea around that drinking a little red wine does you good and protects you from heart disease and other causes of premature death. Sadly this just isn't true and is based on statistical bias in research studies that seemed to show this. It is like the old advertisement for a leading brand of toothpaste that said: 'We took this group of people and asked half of them to brush their teeth with "X". When we followed them up they had significantly fewer fillings and less decay than the half who didn't

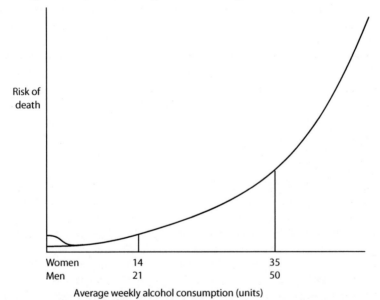

Figure 1.1 Graph of risk of death from cirrhosis vs weekly units drunk[2]

---

[2] The Department of Health has increased the units figure to 28 units a week – not based on new statistics, but on an acceptance of a slightly higher point on the graph as being 'safe'. Then more recently it recommended a daily maximum (2–3 units for women and 3–4 for men) because some people come to harm from more occasional 'binge' drinking.

use "X".' The rumour is that the manufacturers failed to point out that the half who didn't use 'X' had been asked not to brush their teeth at all for a month! This probably isn't true, but it's a good story and illustrates how you can play with statistics.

The same sort of error occurred in the study we are considering. Sure enough, the group who drank a little lived on average longer than those who were teetotal. But think about it for a minute. Who makes up the teetotal group? The answer is that among this group are people who can't drink because they are on medication for heart problems, people who have recently had a heart attack, and people who are recovering from alcoholism. It's hardly surprising that their life expectancy is not quite as good as those without these conditions and it certainly does not show that alcohol is good for you, in however small an amount.

In fact, some recent research has accounted for these factors and still seems to show that red wine in moderation protects against heart disease, but then so does non-alcoholic grape juice. It's a shame, but saying 'I only drink to protect my heart' just doesn't hold water.

What is true, though, is that a small amount of alcohol is not a very big risk at all. It is a sad and strange fact that it is possible to get cirrhosis of the liver even if you have never touched a drop of booze in your life. That strikes me as really unlucky, but fortunately it is extraordinarily rare. You can see from the graph in Figure 1.1 that increasing your drinking up to 14 (21) units weekly increases your risk only very slightly. You may feel that you can't avoid some risk in your life, unless you never leave your bed – and then you would starve to death anyway. So maybe as long as the risk is small it is reasonable.

However, a change happens to the graph at around 14 (21) units weekly. The gradient goes up quite sharply, denoting a rapid increase in risk for increasing consumption above this level. Another change occurs at around 35 (50) units. Above this level every extra drink is causing your risk of death to shoot skywards. At over 100 units weekly the line of risk is somewhere on the second floor above your head.

Of course, these figures are based on whole populations, and so don't tell you what will happen for certain to any particular person. A very few people will be unlucky and come a cropper at relatively low levels of drinking. A few will get away with drinking a lot over a long period. He is usually called Uncle Bill and he is the bane of my life. I am just trying to explain about these risks when someone chirps up, 'But my Uncle Bill drank ten bottles of Scotch a day for 90 years, ran a marathon on his hundredth birthday, and lived to 132.' The point is supposed to be that 'if it's good enough for him, it's good enough for me'. All I can say to this is that for every 'Uncle Bill' who has got away with it, I can sadly show you ten who haven't.

Some of what follows in this book is a bit alarming, particularly what alcohol can do to you. I would like to make sure that you have this in perspective, though. If you drink moderately you can be as sure as you ever can be about anything that you will not come to harm from it.

How should alcohol be used? In my opinion there is only one valid reason for having a drink (at safe levels) and that is social recreation (see Chapter 10). Drinking to help you relax, to sleep, or to give you confidence nearly always leads to problems, because over time you will tend to need more and more to produce the desired effect.

But what if you have had a drink problem in the past and are at present 'on the wagon'. You may feel that what I have said suggests that you can safely go back to drinking, so long as it is below 14 (21) units a week. Unfortunately, it isn't as simple as that.

In my experience very few people who have had a drink problem severe enough to need medical treatment ever manage to return to controlled social drinking – probably 5–10 per cent. In comparison, treatment followed by total abstinence achieves success rates of between 30 and 60–70 per cent, depending on the group studied and the treatment given. Though I am not a betting man, if I had the choice as to which odds to take, I know which I would choose. If we could identify these one in ten people it wouldn't be so bad, but unfortunately it is like the situation bemoaned by the director of Broadmoor hospital a few years ago (the high-security special mental hospital where people who are a danger to society are sent). A reporter asked him why so few people were being discharged. The director replied, 'We could quite safely discharge half of our patients tomorrow. The trouble is, I don't know which half.'

The same problem exists with controlled drinking in people who have suffered from alcoholism. There are a few factors that point to a better than one in ten chance of controlled drinking (see Table 1.2).

Table 1.2 Favourable predictors for controlled drinking

Female
Young (less than 40)
In employment
In supportive relationship
No history of physical addiction to alcohol
Short history of problem drinking (less than a year)

However, these are not very good predictors. Even if you have all of them, your chances of success at controlled drinking don't reach 50/50. If you don't have any of them you have virtually no chance at all. My advice, if you have ever had a drink problem severe enough to require treatment, would be to stick to total abstinence. Don't think of this as a life sentence though. Just take a day at a time. It doesn't mean you can never have fun. Look at people in Alcoholics Anonymous who are in long-term recovery. Are they long-faced and miserable? Are they heck! They're having a ball!

There is another tip about recovery that probably won't please you though: I would advise sticking to soft drinks and avoid alcohol-free lagers or wines. These drinks, though very useful for people trying to cut down their drinking or avoiding drinking and driving, tend not to work for people recovering from alcoholism. They act as a pale imitation of the real thing and are a constant reminder of what you are missing. It is far better to work on finding interests and relaxations that don't involve drinking amber-coloured fluids.

Part 2
WHY DO PEOPLE DRINK TOO MUCH?

2

Causes related to the effects of the drug

The opponent process

Alcohol, like all addictive drugs, undergoes the opponent process. In common with most terms used in psychology, this sounds very complicated, but is in fact very simple. It means that alcohol causes the reverse of its immediate effect in the long term and that the withdrawal effects will be an exaggeration of the long-term effects. Figure 2.1 explains this better than words do.

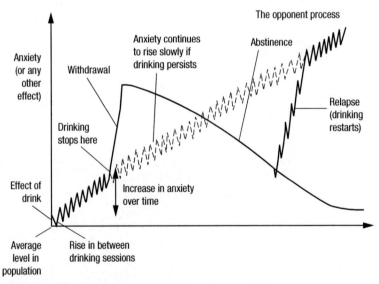

Figure 2.1 The opponent process

We all know and have enjoyed the immediate effects of alcohol. It gives you a lift (raised mood), makes you feel pleasantly calm and relaxed (lowered anxiety), and helps you sleep. It is quite a strong painkiller, and was used in the past as an anaesthetic for major operations. It raises confidence and self-esteem (after a few drinks you feel you could

11

achieve anything, tomorrow). Less well known effects are that it is a muscle relaxant and an anti-epileptic drug. If a person suffering from epilepsy were to have a drink just before a fit was due, the fit might be prevented (unfortunately, this effect is too unpredictable to have any therapeutic usefulness).

From this list we can predict the long-term effects of alcohol used excessively on a daily basis (see Chapter 1 for safe levels of drinking). It will make you depressed (lowered mood), tense and anxious and wreck your sleep. It will give you aches and pains and ruin your confidence and self-esteem. It will give you restless, crampy muscles and, if you are severely addicted, put you at risk of epileptic seizures.

At this point many of my patients smile benignly at me, saying: 'Ah, but doctor, that isn't the case with me. You see, a drink is the only thing that helps me relax; it doesn't make it worse.' A look at Figure 2.1 shows how my patients gain this mistaken impression. The graph shows the effect of alcohol on just one of the aspects mentioned – anxiety – but the same graph would apply for any of the others.

Let's assume that you are more anxious than the average person. If you have a drink, sure enough your anxiety will fall, until the drink wears off, when it goes up again. So you have another drink and your anxiety falls again, until it wears off – so you take another drink and so on. The trouble is that each time the effect of the drink wears off the anxiety rises just a little more than the drink had made it fall. Not enough to be noticeable, but enough to make you significantly more anxious over a period of time than you were before you started drinking.

You are probably not aware of this effect yourself, believing that it is only when you have had enough to give you a hangover that alcohol makes you feel bad. This just isn't the case. I suggest that next week you try an experiment. Every day at lunchtime, rate your anxiety on a scale of 1–10 (1 being the most relaxed that you have ever felt in your life and 10 the most tense) and do the same for your mood (1 = the most depressed and 10 = the most elated in your life). On alternate evenings have a couple or a few drinks; what you would normally have in a light session. On the other nights have nothing to drink at all. You will find that even a couple of drinks makes you more anxious and depressed the next day and that this is easily measurable. The thing is that we don't usually notice it because we assume that it is 'just an off day' or 'I can't have slept well' or some other rationalization. Surely it can't just have been a couple of small gins – except that it can and it was.

My patient's benign smile persists. 'That's all well and good, doctor, but I know that a drink helps me relax because last time I tried without one, I felt terribly tense for several days, and it only went away when I went back to having a drink.' What he is describing is a withdrawal reaction. Withdrawal symptoms start shortly after stopping an addictive drug and go away when the drug is restarted.

By this point (A) you are stuck. If you carry on regularly drinking, your symptoms will gradually get worse. If you don't, they will suddenly get worse. You can't win. Fortunately, there is light at the end of the tunnel. Withdrawal symptoms are short-lived. If you stop drinking completely, your anxiety, or whatever symptom you started drinking to alleviate, will gradually subside, over probably two to six weeks. You will feel better than you have in ages. There is a limit to this, though; it's like the story of the man who injured his hands and asked the doctor, 'Will I be able to play the piano when the bones heal?'

'Oh yes,' says the doctor.

'That's marvellous,' cries the man. 'I've tried for years but never managed it before!'

The old ones are always the best!

Anyway, the point is that your anxiety and other symptoms will only go back to how they were before you started drinking to excess. If you really want to conquer your nerves, you will need to learn the skill of relaxation and practise it. A later chapter may help you with this.

A final cautionary note: the process can restart at any point, but even further accelerated. All that is needed is for you to start drinking regularly again, as Figure 2.1 shows. Once you have developed an alcoholic pattern of drinking, a return to drinking after a period of abstinence (B) leads to a rapid return of symptoms – not at the previous level, but at the level they would have been if you had never stopped drinking. This is why Alcoholics Anonymous and others see alcoholism as a progressive and incurable disease. The underlying disease process seems to be continuing. Once contracted, the only way to avoid the symptoms is to abstain from alcohol, in which case you will be fine.

Exceptional traits

Every human feature that varies continuously in the population, such as height, weight, intelligence, or talent at removing the top from a Schweppes tonic bottle without having it explode in your face, is distributed in the same way. This is shown in Figure 2.2 on page 14 and is known as a 'normal distribution curve'.

Lots of people are in the middle of this curve and very few are right at the ends. For example, lots of people are between 5ft and 6ft 6in tall. Very few are below 4ft 6in or above 7ft, but a few are. People at the ends

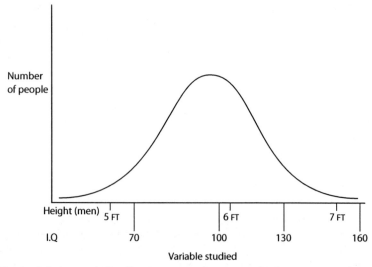

Figure 2.2 Normal distribution curve for a population

of this curve tend to suffer problems associated with this exceptional trait. This is easy to see for very tall or very short people, but it applies to other traits too. For example, very intelligent people suffer a higher incidence of mental illness than the rest of us.

If you are at the end of the distribution curve for a trait that has a link of any sort with drinking, you may be at risk of developing a problem with alcohol. To use an earlier example, if you are much more anxious than the average, you may be at risk because of the temptation to use alcohol as a short-term tranquillizer, and we have seen the problems that can lead to. Incidentally, you wouldn't have thought that people with very low levels of anxiety would have a problem, but they do. They are called psychopaths. These people, not having the advantage of anxiety as a check against excesses or a warning of impending danger, get into a lot of trouble and cause people around them considerable grief.

Anyway, I digress. Many other traits are relevant here. For example, what if, for you, alcohol is exceptionally effective in relieving anxiety, or lifting mood? For me, being probably average in this regard, it works a bit, but not much. If I'm really tense or miserable, it doesn't help at all. If it is amazingly effective (in the short term) for you, you may be at risk. What if, for you, drinking is the most pleasurable activity imaginable? I quite enjoy a drink, but again being boringly average, it isn't for me the bee's knees. There are several other activities I prefer, though I would rather keep the details to myself.

I could go on, but I think I can leave you to work out what are your exceptional traits and whether any of them have a link with alcohol and drinking. The implication is obvious. You may need to work on these traits and develop coping strategies other than drinking to manage them. This may mean seeking professional advice, or may be resolvable through the support of friends and family. In my experience, friends are a much underused resource. We tend to spare them the burden of sharing our problems, while most of us like nothing more than to be confided in and to feel helpful. A few hints here for the recipient of these confidences. It is better to listen and invite more by sympathetic attention than to leap in with premature advice or, folly of follies, to offer a parallel experience of your own. When advice is needed you will be asked for it directly. Never say 'Oh well, I'm sure it will turn out all right in the end' or, worst of all, 'Pull yourself together.' These sorts of statements say in effect to the confider, 'Take your problems away, they are too painful, I don't want them.' A warm, attentive silence, with the odd word here and there to encourage him to continue, says on the contrary, 'Give me more of your problems, I can handle it and would like to share the burden with you.'

Increased salience

Alcohol is again like many other addictive drugs in having the property of increasing in importance, over time, to the regular user. Some other drugs can be even worse at this, though alcohol is pretty bad. A man addicted to heroin once said to me, 'Heroin is like my mistress, but she is the most demanding mistress a man could have. She takes up my every waking moment and my every thought.' Ignoring the possibly sexist overtones in this statement, I think that this was a beautiful description of the experience of taking an addictive drug. This chap, who had recently succeeded in kicking the habit, was depressed. He summed his problem up thus: 'Once you have had heroin, nothing in life can ever measure up to the experience of that first fix. Life from then on is a disappointment. How can I enjoy a walk through the grass on a spring morning again? It just isn't as good as heroin.' This is why addictive drugs can ruin your life. Alcohol does not do this after a few doses, like heroin, but it can if used to excess over a long period. There is in fact evidence that alcohol and other addictive drugs work on a part of the brain known as the pleasure centre. Initially they switch it on, but over time they make it less sensitive, making it very difficult to get pleasure from anything.

An example of this phenomenon for a problem drinker would be his reaction if you invited him to accompany you to the theatre. Instead of 'Yes, I would love to', he will say something like 'Yes, OK, but is there a bar there?' Having satisfied himself on this point, he will find out when the bar opens and ensure that you get there early enough to have a couple of drinks before the performance. He will be an expert at how to get drinks ordered in advance for the interval, so that valuable drinking time is not lost queuing. He will also make sure that the performance finishes well before closing-time and will have reconnoitred the area in advance to find the nearest pub. In reality, the play was only a vehicle for his main concern, which was to maintain a high blood alcohol concentration.

In Figure 2.3, circle 1 represents a hypothetical person's life. This circle represents the boundaries of his life. The nearer the centre of the

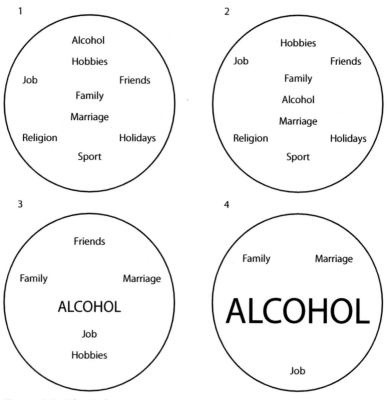

Figure 2.3 Life circles

circle a particular aspect is, the more central and important it is to him. Every person would have a different pattern in his circle, but this chap is not untypical of many of us.

In circle 1 alcohol is a fairly peripheral part of his life. But alcohol has the property that, if you drink enough of it for long enough, it will start to move to the centre of the circle. Once there, (circle 2), it will displace what was holding the central position. It then grows, (circle 3), and continues to do so until it takes up almost the whole area (circle 4).

As you can see, in this man's life, most things have been lost through having been squeezed out by alcohol. Family, marriage and job are just hanging on, but they too will be forced out soon.

What if, in the nick of time, this man recognizes the disaster that is occurring, decides to stop drinking, and maybe get treatment to help him do so? What is left?

As you can see from Figure 2.4, his life is now very empty, with a gaping hole in the middle. The implication here is that he is going to need to fill this gap as a matter of urgency. This may take a lot of work, because many of the aspects lost from his life may not be easy to get back. He may need to re-evaluate his life, asking himself some pretty fundamental questions, such as 'What are the purposes and reasons for my life?' Until his decision to stop drinking, he was living for instant gratification in the form of the next drink.

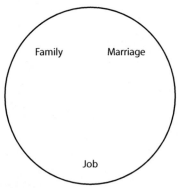

Figure 2.4 Empty life circle

But if he fails to fill this gap in his life, there is one thing that will fit the space perfectly, like a glove. I needn't spell this out, but I would urge anyone who stops drinking after a period of excess to take some time out to think.

Awareness reduction

One of alcohol's effects, which makes it such a popular recreational drug, is that it reduces your awareness. At a dinner party, you will regale your neighbour with a story of your recent holiday, noting with wonder how sparkling and informative your account is. Only the next morning do you see the truth when your wife points out that the victim of your discourse fell asleep halfway through your first week at the Bonaventure Hotel. Poor chap had to go to the bathroom when his head fell in his trifle.

Even quite small amounts of alcohol have this effect. In an experiment with bus drivers attempting to negotiate their buses through traffic cones on a skid pan, half were given one pint of beer prior to the test, while the others were deprived of this. The beer drinkers assessed their performance as significantly superior to the norm, whereas in fact they had performed significantly worse than their sober colleagues.

More serious things happen if you use alcohol regularly to excess.

Drinking will lower your performance. You may make some bad mistakes with serious consequences, or make a fool of yourself. When you sober up, this realization hurts. You now have two choices. You can put up with this pain and work extra hard to put the damage right. Alternatively, and more simply, you can get drunk. The pain will subside and you will begin to see your actions in a rosy glow. 'I'm not so bad. It's all their fault for being so critical. Why shouldn't a guy have a drink, anyway?' The problem with this strategy is that you are

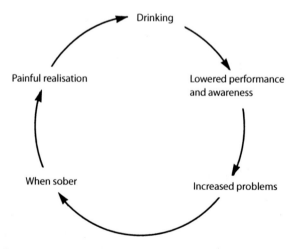

Figure 2.5 Awareness reduction

now trapped. If you continue drinking, your performance gets even worse and you dig an even bigger hole for yourself. If you sober up, the realization of the mess you have made of things is even worse. 'Oh, no. What have I done?' you think. The pain and remorse is unbearable. So you have another drink and the worry goes away. It stays away so long as you carry on drinking. There is no logical end to this downward spiral.

Let's face it, sooner or later you are going to have to come to terms with the situation you have created (see Figure 2.5). The sooner this is, the easier it will be. You will need lots of support. A word to partners here: you may well have been through hell while the drinking was going on, but this is not the time for recriminations. It takes a load of guts to face the pain of self-realization, warts and all, and you can help a lot by recognizing this. I will refer to the organizations Alcoholics Anonymous and Al-Anon a little later; they can be very helpful at this time.

A little bit of self-righteousness does not go amiss at this stage. In my experience, the most successful people at giving up drugs, alcohol or cigarettes are often those who become evangelists for the cause. An example is the reformed smoker who gives his still smoking peers a tough time concerning their habit. If you have done something difficult and worthwhile, then why not flaunt it?

3

Causes related to past experience

Social learning theory

Dozens of books much longer than this one have been written on social learning theory, so what I am going to say can only touch superficially on one aspect as it relates to excessive drinking. However, like all the theories listed in this chapter, it has relevance to some people; and for them, it also holds important implications.

Let's imagine ourselves in an animal experimentation laboratory. Fortunately, to my knowledge this experiment is no longer carried out as it is rather unpleasant, but the result has been confirmed many times.

An animal, such as a mouse, is placed in a cage with an electrified floor. Every ten seconds the mouse receives an electric shock. The mouse looks round the cage for a way out, but finds none. It sees a bar (no, not one with drinks on it) at the end of the cage and eventually it presses it. The next shock is prevented by the bar being pressed, as it is linked to the electricity supply in such a way that this stops the flow of current for ten seconds. When the mouse fails to press the bar it receives another shock, but it soon learns to press the bar regularly to avoid it. By increasing the presses necessary to prevent the shocks, the mouse can be made to do enough work to illuminate a light bulb. Another way of getting the mouse to do this work is to put a needle into one of its veins and to inject a drug each time it presses the bar. If the drug injected is heroin, the mouse will work incredibly hard to get more of the drug. It won't stop until it lapses into a coma or dies of exhaustion. Though not quite so spectacular, it will work quite hard for alcohol too. Other favourites are stimulants such as cocaine. Tranquillizers such as Valium or Ativan are not so effective, and the mouse won't lift a paw to get a dose of LSD.

So the mouse learns to work for a reward or for the avoidance of punishment. But what if we are now really nasty and uncouple the bar from the electric supply so the mouse can no longer stop the shocks by bar-pressing? It will be unpleasantly surprised, but it will work even harder for a while to try to stop the shocks, assuming it isn't doing enough. Eventually it will get the message and give up. After a while of desperate searching for a way out, it will lie on the floor of the cage motionless and accept whatever shocks come to it. If the door of the cage is then opened, the mouse will remain lying there and will have to be brought out. A fierce and hungry cat is then let into the room. The mouse will lie where it is and let itself be eaten.

This animal has learned to be helpless. It has learned that 'whatever I do I can't influence what happens to me. From time to time something nasty is going to happen. I might just as well curl up and accept it.'

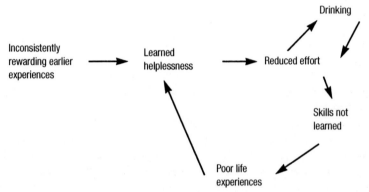

Figure 3.1 The development of learned helplessness

This is the phenomenon of 'learned helplessness' (Figure 3.1) and it can happen to any animal, even a human. Professional torturers learn early in their careers how to induce this state by making their victims feel powerless to influence what happens to them.

Let us now change the scene to a room with a little girl in it. She is busily drawing a picture for her daddy. Please excuse the stereotypes here, but for the purpose of this example Mummy is at home and Daddy is out at work. The little girl is lavishing great care on the picture because she wants Daddy to be pleased. It is a good picture, and as the time approaches for Daddy to come home she is getting more and more excited. I can't wait to see his face when he sees my picture, he will be so pleased, she thinks.

A key turns in the lock and Daddy comes in. The little girl rushes up to him, holding out her picture and shouting, 'Daddy, Daddy, Daddy, look what I've drawn for you. Do you like it, Daddy?'

But Daddy is drunk. The last thing that he needs right now is a screaming kid getting in his way; he's going to bed. He throws aside the picture and shoves away the little girl. 'Leave me alone, you little pest,' he slurs as he weaves up the stairs. She is left sobbing on the floor, her hopes crumpled up with her picture.

The next day she is really naughty. She does nothing to help her mother and is rude and disobedient. Why shouldn't she be? Being good didn't lead to much. However, as the time approaches for her father's return she becomes apprehensive as she realizes she has been bad.

But Daddy is feeling very guilty about the night before and so when he gets in he goes up to the little girl and hugs and kisses her saying, 'You are the best little girl in the whole world, you are so good and I love you.'

Hang on, thinks the girl, I've been bad all day. She is very confused.

It doesn't need this chaotic and unpredictable pattern to happen long before the little girl learns to be helpless. 'Whatever I do, I can't control what is going to happen to me. Sometimes it will be nasty and sometimes it will be nice, but I have no influence on the world and how it treats me.' She gives up and accepts the slings and arrows of outrageous fortune without question or effort.

How will she grow up? Well, as she has given up she will not put herself in a position to learn from experience. I don't just mean academically here. She won't put effort into relationships, interests and building a complete life for herself either. Essentially, by giving up she insulates herself from emotional risks: 'If I don't try I can never fail.'

As she gets older, drinking may become an outward manifestation of this helplessness. Hiding in the bottle allows her to forget how far behind she has fallen. A vicious circle has started by now. Because she has put nothing in, she gets nothing out of life and she learns nothing. Her skills and confidence fall further. This confirms her negative view of the world and she gives up even more, retreating further into the bottle.

And so an alcoholic life is set up.

How does she get out of this hole? Of course, she is going to need help, probably through therapy, but what must she do herself? You may have your own ideas, but to me the essential element is deciding to take emotional risks. This may seem strange to suggest to someone who is taking great risks with her health through drinking, but withdrawing into helplessness is really a way of being safe from being told your efforts are not good enough.

There is a link here with depression. Some psychiatrists see depression as being the human equivalent of hibernation in animals, having been passed on in some humans through their genes from their animal ancestors. When an animal faces very harsh circumstances with which it cannot cope, it withdraws into hibernation, waking up when conditions improve. In depression the same happens, the difference being that it is accompanied by terrible suffering. Maybe this is the price we have paid as a species for the development of our intellectual capacity.

In order to achieve anything, we have to be able to fail. Imagine a lad turning up to a party. He thinks, I mustn't let myself be rejected, I just couldn't bear it. So he goes and stands by the bar all evening, making himself as inconspicuous as possible. All evening he watches people dancing and at the end he goes home to bed. He has succeeded in avoiding being rejected.

Another lad goes into the party and walks straight up to the first girl who looks nice. 'Would you like a dance?' he asks hopefully.

'What, with you? Not likely, you're spotty and ugly. Go away.'

So he walks up to another promising girl. 'Would you dance with me?'

'No. I wouldn't be seen dead with you. You smell. Get lost.'

He tries again with another girl and this time gets a different response:

'Yes, I'd love to. Thank you.'

They have a great evening and strike up a friendship. I will resist the temptation to develop this romantic tale further here, but I would ask this: only one of these boys avoided rejection and failure, but who achieved more?

To return to our little girl, now adult. In my view, her only route to a happy and fulfilled life is through accepting that she will fail some of the time if she tries things; quite a lot at first and less often as time goes on. If she can forgive herself these failures and keep on going, she will learn from her experiences, gain skills and, with them, confidence. Mistakes are great; they are how we learn, so long as we honestly acknowledge them and treat ourselves respectfully when we make them. Don't let yourself get away with critical self-talk such as 'How could I have done that, I'm such an idiot'.

I am constantly surprised by how many of my patients identify with this tragic tale, recounting stories similar in almost every detail. Others develop learned helplessness later in life, through repeated traumas, losses or abusive relationships. Though it is much easier to induce learned helplessness in children than in adults, even adults can become helpless if traumatized enough. The result is the same; if this pattern applies to you, you can do something about it. It isn't too late.

Psychoanalytic theories

If a lot has been written on social learning theory, I could fill several libraries with the works of psychoanalysts. Again, you will need to read more detailed texts if you are interested in this side of things.

Sigmund Freud is the father of psychoanalysis. You need to take some of what he wrote with a pinch of salt, and some of it seems a little bizarre, but he made an enormous contribution to psychology and within what he said lie some very profound truths.

Freud realized that all humans are motivated by drives. He felt that two main drives are elaborated, as life goes on, to produce the whole range of human behaviour. One is the Life Drive or 'libido' and the other the Death Drive. The Life Drive will motivate a person to compete and be productive. In times past the person with the greatest Life Drive would be the one who remained alive to pass on his genes, through his skills in procuring food and in running away from sabre-tooth tigers. He would also have the most successful sex life, causing a lot of new life to be formed. Nowadays the libido has come to be taken as meaning just the sex drive. It is more than that, but Freud recognized that sexuality is linked up with most human behaviour.

He also felt that the libido is present from birth and that even children possess sexuality, though in a different form from that of adults. This drive passes through various phases as the child gets older.

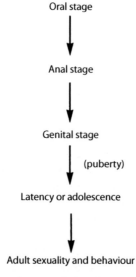

Figure 3.2 Stages of psychosexual development

The first is the Oral stage (see Figure 3.2). This is the phase during which the baby is totally preoccupied with warmth, security and feeding. It is a wondrous thing to behold the effect of the mother's breast (or a feeding bottle) on a hungry infant. The child is screaming his little lungs out. I don't know about you, but this sound has always seemed to me to come straight from the bowels of hell. He is purple with agitation, frustration and rage. Mum comes along, picks him up, and puts him on the breast. Within half a second he is the picture of perfect contentment and utter bliss. He is warm, secure, gratified and at peace with the world. This never ceases to amaze me. How can he do it, and so quickly? But, for the baby, life is not so complex as it will later become. It is purely a matter of knowing that his needs will be met, that when he cries, mum will be there, dependable as ever, that she will cuddle him, make him feel nice and secure, and will make the nasty hungry feeling in his stomach go away, by letting him suck on that nice warm breast or teat.

Observing him at play, you will see him put everything in his mouth. His mouth is the core of his being; it is what he is about.

What, though, if Mum has a drink problem, or for some other reason cannot be relied upon to be there when needed? Incidentally, there is no evidence that Dad can't fulfil this function satisfactorily. He has an anatomical disadvantage, but that isn't the point; he can cuddle and coo and hold the bottle instead of Mum if necessary. But if nobody is reliably there, the baby will not learn that the world is a good, safe, dependable place where you can be sure that your needs will be gratified. Like many other aspects outlined in this book, this should be kept in perspective. Occasionally leaving the baby crying for a while is not going to do any harm. Indeed at some point or other he is going to have to learn to tolerate frustration, and this time is as good as any. The important thing is that the baby learns to expect that his needs will be met eventually, even if sometimes this will involve a wait.

Freud stated that a child can only pass on to the next stage of development of the libido once the previous one has been safely taken on board. If for any reason this is disrupted, then the child will become arrested at this level of development. If nothing happens to allow him to catch up on this at a later stage, he will remain fixated on this aspect of life right into adulthood.

If the Oral stage is successfully passed, the child will pass to the Anal stage of development. This is the stage of potty training. The child learns here that he can control those around him and make things happen, just by opening his bowels or refusing to do so. He can make his parents very pleased or very cross, and whatever they may try to do about it, he remains in control. It is normal for there to be a bit of a struggle between parent and child at this stage, but at the end of it all the child should feel, 'Hey! I can make things happen!' Freud thought that if anything disrupted this phase the result would be an adult fixated at the Anal stage, obsessed with control and retention, tending to hoard money and possessions and being obsessional in habits.

Next is the Genital stage (see Figure 3.3). This is when the child realizes he has a part of his body that feels particularly nice when he fiddles with it. Consequently he does practically nothing else. If left with his peers he will talk mostly of willies, poo, wee-wee, or whatever word is used locally for female external genitalia. This will cause great hilarity and bears endless repetition.

Figure 3.3 Coping with genital stage children

This can be a testing and occasionally embarrassing time for parents, requiring the setting down of limits on behaviour without making the child feel that his body or sexual organs are dirty or things to be ashamed of. If there are problems at this stage, the resulting adult will tend to have difficulties recognizing sexual experience as something to be shared. Relationships will tend to be shallow and self-centred.

There follow a number of less well-defined stages, including the traumas of puberty and adolescence which we all know about, culminating in the development of mature adult drives and sexuality.

To return to the Oral stage. If this stage is not successfully encountered, the outcome will be an adult whose life is fixated upon the instant gratification of needs and impulses. He will crave emotional warmth and security. He will need a lot of reassurance and will tend to see the world as a hostile place full of dangers and pitfalls. He will not be able to tolerate frustration. The best way to find this warmth, security and reassurance is through a mutually giving relationship, but this won't work for him. He needs to get rid of any nasty feelings and he needs it NOW. There is nothing that can do this for you except a drug, and alcohol does it as well as any. I have talked before about the warm cosy glow that drinking produces in the early stages. This is just what a person fixated at the Oral stage of development craves. This person, if he wishes to conquer his drink problem, is going to need to search for other ways of gaining gratification and to work on coping with uncertainty and emotional discomfort without trying to chase them away. It is a truism, but often ignored, that if you are feeling bad one day, you don't have to do anything about it. If you stay with the feelings and don't use alcohol, sleeping tablets or whatever else to abolish them, they will eventually go away and stay away. 'I'll feel better tomorrow' is nearly always true. Of course, I am not talking here of someone with a depressive illness or suffering grief, but even in the latter case this principle of 'working through' emotional pain, rather than avoiding it, works.

Another, more recent psychoanalytic theory that concentrates on the baby and his relationships with his parents is that of Narcissism (see Figure 3.4).

Babies do not recognize the existence of other people as such. They see them as objects in a strange world that they have been catapulted

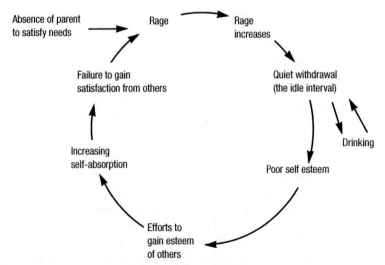

Figure 3.4 Narcissistic personality development

into, but they do not see them as whole persons with needs and feelings of their own.

Babies are entirely self-centred, as many an exasperated parent will know. They see their mother, or their closest parent, as a reflection of themselves. It is this relationship with a close and attentive mother that first focuses the baby's attention on the outside world. He sees his mother most of the time as being good, and reflected in her he sees that he must be good too. In due course he will come to recognize his mother as separate from him and will start to understand that other people exist. He can tolerate this because he has got a good image of himself tucked inside his head.

However, if his mother is not attentive, comforting and rewarding to the baby – for example, if she does not come to his cry – things happen differently. At first, he will become enraged and scream his head off. Eventually, his anger, frustration and despair grow too great. He copes with this by rejecting the outside world, including his mother, and becomes quietly self-absorbed. He looks like a very well-behaved baby, but an astute observer will notice that he is not interested in anyone around him. He does not see his mother as 'good', and in mirroring her he does not see himself as good either. As he grows up he may make friends, but his relationships tend to be pretty shallow. He tends to use people and is unable to understand or react to their feelings or needs.

As a grown-up, this person has no inner feeling of himself as a good or worthwhile person. He desperately craves praise for himself, while being unable to give it to others. Tragically, he misses the fact that we only get rewards from other people if we are rewarding to them. He tries harder and harder to get the applause he wants and becomes rather tiresome with his self-centredness. The situation he suffered as a baby is re-created, with people increasingly shunning him. Again he becomes enraged and eventually abandons any attempt to interact meaningfully with people altogether, growing even more inward-looking. He finds solace in internal feelings and sensations and he craves tranquillity and insulation from external demands. This craving for tranquillity links in with theories concerning the Death Drive (see below).

This is where alcohol (or other drugs) come in. They provide a short-term way of feeling good inside and excluding the outside world with which he cannot cope. So begins his route to alcoholism.

While most of us have a part that is narcissistic (that is, self-absorbed and self-centred), we are aware of it, feel a bit guilty about it, and soon recognize the need to look outwards and attend to other people's feelings too. The true narcissist does not.

This history and picture is one that I see quite often in alcoholic and drug-abusing patients.

An art therapist colleague has made a study of pictures drawn by some of these individuals. The most common, occurring amazingly frequently, is a picture of a tropical beach, with golden sand, sea and palm trees in the sun, but no people, apart maybe from a waiter serving drinks (see Figure 3.5). Typically the person doing the drawing will comment, 'I just want to feel good, with nobody hassling me.'

Figure 3.5 Palm trees in the sun – an alcoholic patient's picture

So what is this unhappy person to do? I think that the key is in looking for ways to gain self-esteem. If he feels really good about himself, he has no need to show off or be self-obsessed and will become more popular and gain more real praise as a result. This can be gained through therapy, by striving for achievement, by helping others, or by joining a group and sharing in their self-valuing (support of a football club is a good example of this). The essence is learning to concentrate on other people, rather than yourself.

Again I must stress here that no parent can be perfect and attentive all the time; indeed, this is neither needed nor helpful. What is needed is to be 'good enough' to be seen by the baby as lovable and worth-while, and so to give him the feeling that he must be worthwhile too.

Earlier on I mentioned the Death Drive. Freud and other psychoanalysts felt that there is a balance between this and the Life Drive in each person (see Figure 3.6 on page 30).

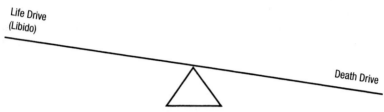

Figure 3.6 The balance between Life and Death Drives

If you doubt that the drive towards death exists, I would invite you to take a trip around the M25. Every few miles someone in a 7 series BMW will come up behind you and settle 3½ inches from your rear bumper. He ignores the fact that you are both travelling at 70 miles an hour and that there is a line of traffic 10 miles long ahead. Even if he passed you it would take him an hour to get past the line of cars in your vision. He is presumably not stupid (though I concede that ownership of a BMW is no guarantee of intellect), so he must know that if anything unexpected happens on the motorway he is going to die. Why on earth does he do it?

The answer is simple. Because it's fun. You never feel quite as alive as when you are playing with death. The nearness of it is thrilling, though frightening at the same time. That is why people jump out of aeroplanes or climb mountains. Paradoxically, the Death Drive also represents a yearning for tranquillity; the peace of the inorganic quietude of death.

Some psychoanalysts see abuse of alcohol or drugs as a reflection of a predominance of the Death Drive over the Life Drive. The insulation from the realities of life when drunk can be seen as a link to the quietness of death and, indeed, repeated heavy drinking brings you nearer to death all the time.

If this makes some sense to you in terms of your make-up, it may be worth, first, finding more productive and rewarding ways of dicing with death, and second, looking at the competitive, productive parts of yourself (your Life Drive) and working on developing these areas of your life, and third, looking for other ways of finding peace and tranquillity.

More recently psychoanalysts have pointed out another phenomenon that may lead to heavy drinking or other problems later in life. Let's go back to the little girl we looked at in the section on social learning theory. She is now between five and eight years old. It is at this age that identification happens. A little girl will tend to copy her mother, performing her actions in miniature. With apologies again for the stereotype, a little boy will be carefully changing a tyre on his toy truck while his father is doing the same on the family car. Indeed, it is probably at this age that sex stereotypes are handed on from one generation to the next. At the same time children are identifying with their school friends, forming into gangs and making 'best friends'. They will tend to behave, dress and look the same way. They are beginning to develop an image of who they are and what they are like.

But our little girl is being treated badly by her dad. She feels, 'I must be bad. I must be really horrible if dad treats me this way.' To her, adults – and especially her parents – are always right. If Dad tells her she is bad, hits her and abuses her, then she must be. She has great problems with the process of identification: 'I'm not like any of my friends at school, they are nice and their daddies don't hit them.' So she can't identify and feel like them. 'I'm not like Mummy, because she is nice and kind and clever; Daddy says I am stupid.' She can't identify with her mum, and the same applies to anyone that she likes and admires.

But there is one person with whom she can identify, because, like her, he is nasty, has obvious weaknesses, and she hates him: her dad (see Figure 3.7).

As children get older, they tend to become more and more like the people with whom they identify, often their parents. It has long been assumed that most children go through a stage of rebellion during

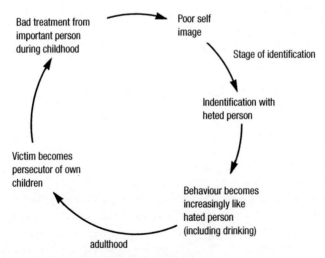

Figure 3.7 Identification with the hated person

adolescence, when they reject their parents' values and everything they stand for. In fact, in most cases the opposite occurs and adolescents are often mirrors of their parents' views and attitudes.

Our little girl, without realizing it, becomes more and more like her father as she grows up. Inevitably and inexorably she starts drinking in her teens and does so to excess. She becomes unpredictable and argumentative. When she has children, she finds herself from time to time treating them unkindly and notes with distress their reaction to her drunkenness. This awakens in her hazy memories of her own feelings as a child, but she doesn't know why she acts this way and isn't able to change. Occasionally she will remark, 'Oh no. I'm turning out just like my dad. How could I? I hate him.'

And so the pattern of unhappy drinking is passed down the generations. Of course, this is only an example. The collapse of self-esteem and subsequent identification with the tormentor can be caused by anyone, whether relation, acquaintance or teacher, and boys are every bit as vulnerable as girls; but a stable, loving home life is very protective. A child who feels special, good, loved and needed at home is likely to be pretty choosy about who she identifies with.

The reason why this theory seems so important to me, apart from the fact that it clearly applies to many of my patients, is that awareness of what has happened and is happening is the biggest part of putting things right. Once you are aware that many of the things you do that you would rather not do are a reflection of the person you like and admire the least, you are able to reject them if you wish: 'No, I don't want to be my dad, I am me.' Consciously rejecting that person's behaviour and values is very worthwhile. Changing your own behaviour is difficult but, as I will explain later, can be done through practice.

Self-handicapping

Another shift of scene now to the home of a boy whose parents are very different from those described before. They are never nasty or cruel to him. They certainly never get drunk. They are studious, hard-working, honourable and rather reserved. The boy gets little criticism, but little praise either. His parents feel that they are very good to him, giving him lots of presents, dressing him well, instilling in him all the right values and ensuring that he has a good education. They try to do everything for him that a parent could do.

But that is the problem: they do lots for him but have forgotten what he can do for them. The little boy feels bombarded by beneficence but feels completely unable to please or impress his parents. He doesn't feel very important or good about himself.

Then the first major exam comes up at school. He works hard for it, as he has been taught to do. When the result arrives he has done very well. His parents are delighted. For the first time in his life he is made to feel king of the world. The feeling is intoxicating and he is hooked. He needs more.

So he keeps it up and, in fact, redoubles his efforts. This goes on all through his schooling. He does well, gets a good job, and achieves everything that is expected of him, but all the time has to work harder to keep up. He must, because he couldn't bear to endure the disappointment of parents and contemporaries if he were to fail.

He is promoted quite fast, but as he rises up the company he is beginning to struggle to keep up with what is required of him. Then he realizes an awful fact: his colleagues, with whom he is competing for advancement, are more able than him. They are achieving more with a fraction of the effort. So he redoubles his efforts again to keep up. But his latest promotion was the final straw. Even by working all the hours that God gives he cannot deliver the goods. In addition, his relationships suffer.

He is now trapped in a nightmare (see Figure 3.8).

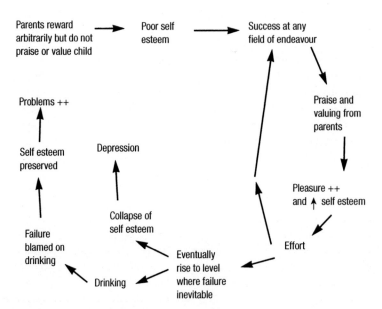

Figure 3.8 Self-handicapping

He has only two obvious choices. Either he tries to work even harder, in which case he will break down, or he fails. But to him, failure would be worse than death. It would be the death of his self-esteem, which has no other base than his constant injections of success.

There is another way out, though. He drinks. He complains of the stress he is under, and understandably needs something to help him relax. His drinking eventually escalates to such a level that he loses his job. He sits at home and broods, 'If it wasn't for the booze, you know, I could have been managing director.'

Despite the disaster that has befallen him, his self-esteem has escaped more or less intact. He has been able to handicap himself in order to get out of his trap, and has managed to pin the reason on to an agent external to himself, thus preserving his vision of himself as someone who can always succeed.

It's a high price to pay, though.

What else could he do? Well, this is going to take a lot of work, of a different kind, and I certainly wouldn't suggest that it is easy. He will have to make a total reappraisal of himself and his life. He is a worthwhile person, but what is it that makes him so? What are his most important qualities and attributes? What are the purposes of his life? Is it OK to do something worthwhile, but not necessarily be the absolute top? Is it OK to try something and fail? I have already discussed the merits of tolerating failure, so you know my views on that. I will look more at the concept of 'OK-ness' a bit later on. In the meantime, our subject is going to need a lot of support and affirmation that he is a valuable person independent of his material success.

Incidentally, I have used an example of career success. The same principle can apply to any other form of endeavour – for example, in forming relationships, developing prowess at sports, being musical or, in fact, anything that leads to parental or societal approval. The process and the answers are the same whatever the field.

4

Family, personality and other causes

Transactional Analysis theory

Transactional Analysis is a way of looking at human behaviour; it was first described by Eric Berne, an American psychologist. His book *Games People Play* is not only a very readable bestseller, but is also in my view one of the most important pieces of psychology ever written. I strongly recommend that you read it, as I can only give a very short and pale version of the real thing in this chapter. Much of what I will describe is a simplification of what Berne described, and my description of the 'Alcoholic Game' is substantially different from what you will find in *Games People Play*. While it leans heavily on Berne's work, I have altered the description of the game to fit the pattern that I have observed in some of my patients. I would caution here that you may feel that some of this theory as it applies to people with drink problems is cynical and pejorative. I can only say that it isn't meant that way, but Berne's clear observation and forthright style pull no punches and are designed to help people who are in trouble with their lives to achieve greater happiness and fulfilment. In my description I have the same aim.

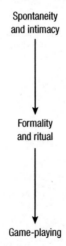

Spontaneity
and intimacy

Formality
and ritual

Game-playing

Figure 4.1 Levels of relationships

35

This theory sees relationships as existing on at least three possible levels. The most advanced level is that of spontaneity and intimacy. Spontaneity is saying what you feel as you feel it, in a straightforward way, and also living each moment as it comes. Intimacy is sharing your experience and feelings openly with the person you are relating to (see Figure 4.1).

This is clearly a desirable level of relationship in a marriage, but would not always be possible or reasonable in every situation. For example, if on the first occasion that I met you I was to advance and kiss you, you would rightly be appalled. It would probably confirm the view you always had of psychiatrists and you would conclude that I was a bit strange.

It is for situations such as this that the next level of relationship exists – that is formality and ritual. Formality is the creation of a certain emotional distance and the setting of boundaries to behaviour that are accepted by both parties. Ritual is the carrying out of prescribed rules, symbolic acts and patterns of behaviour that may have no practical purpose in themselves, but make the relationship safe. For example, on first meeting you, I would probably hold out my hand to shake yours and say, 'Hello, how do you do?' I don't expect a real answer to this query; in fact, I would be nonplussed if you were to reply, 'Well, not too good really. I'm having trouble with the mortgage and the dog was sick on the carpet this morning.' This would be too spontaneous and intimate for the situation. An answer such as 'Fine, thank you, nice to meet you' will do excellently, even if in truth it is extremely tiresome to have had to come and meet me. These rituals protect us all and make the world go round. However, if a marriage exists on this level, something is wrong and neither partner is likely to be happy.

There are rare exceptions, such as the patient whom I asked about his marriage.

'Oh, it's just fine,' he replied.

'Good,' I said, 'because your GP says in his letter that you weren't speaking.'

'We aren't.'

'Well, when did you last talk to your wife?'

'Three years ago.'

Though this man was satisfied with the lack of communication with his spouse so long as she cooked his supper and did the chores, most of us need more to be fulfilled.

The lowest level of relationship in this hierarchy is game-playing. In this context games are not amusing pastimes. They can be trivial or serious, and at the extreme can even lead to death. A game is a covert interaction in which what is said is not what is meant, but is a way of putting the person to whom you are relating in a position he would not otherwise accept. This is done for some psychological or actual gain, the so-called 'pay-off'.

Virtually all of us play games from time to time, usually without realizing we are doing it. We aren't trying to be devious or nasty, it's just a habit we have got into over the years.

For example, almost all of you will at some point have played a variant of this game . . . I have a bad day at work. A couple of difficult patients criticize my treatment and are impossible to satisfy. I can't snipe back at them; that wouldn't be very professional. So I smile and hold on to my irritation. In addition, one of the hospital managers gives me an extra load of paperwork to deal with and a GP rings up to complain that he hasn't received a discharge letter yet, which was due three years ago. When I get home I am ready to fire off at somebody, anybody.

'Hello, darling, have you had a good day?'

'Humphh.'

'Oh dear, are you all right?'

'Yes, I'm fine' (through clenched teeth).

'Are you sure? You seem very tense.'

'Yes, I'm fine. I'm fine, OK? Now will you please stop quizzing me. I didn't expect the damned Spanish Inquisition.'

Very wisely, the matter is allowed to drop and a brooding silence ensues.

An hour later you have had enough.

'Oh, come on, you haven't said a thing all evening.'

'Well, you haven't even asked me about it. I've had a bloody awful day and you can't even be bothered to talk to me about it. It'd be nice to get a bit of support around here.'

Now, there is no point at all in getting involved in this sort of discussion, but unless you are a canonized saint, you do.

So I have my argument and am able to offload all the frustration and anger of the day on to you. I feel a lot better and you feel that somehow you have been put upon.

A common type of domestic game. If it happens occasionally, it is part of the hurly-burly of everyday life in a close relationship, but if the whole relationship is based on an intricate game or set of games, serious consequences ensue.

Before going any further, I should explain that Berne saw relationships as also occurring on another axis with three levels. These involve the roles of parent, adult and child.

In Figure 4.2 both parties are relating to each other as adults and

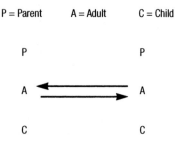

Figure 4.2 Adult–Adult relationship

there is no problem. However, in Figure 4.3 one partner is treating the other as a parent would treat a child, while the latter wants an adult–adult relationship.

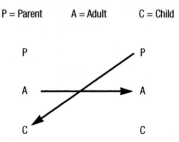

Figure 4.3 A crossed interaction

Like any relationship in which the lines cross, there will be open conflict here and maybe game-playing too.

A much more stable situation occurs if the lines are parallel, as in Figure 4.4, though the relationship will not be very productive and mutual game-playing will be needed to maintain the status quo.

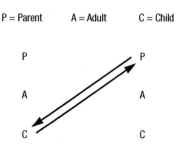

Figure 4.4 A parallel interaction

The so-called 'Alcoholic Game' (see Figure 4.5) is set up for just this purpose. I must stress again here that this is not exactly the game

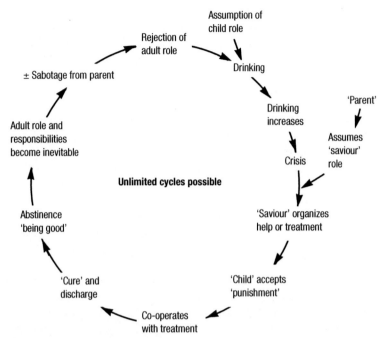

Figure 4.5 The 'Alcoholic Game'

described by Berne but is my variation, based on my personal observation of some alcoholic relationships.

One partner has taken up the child role. Let's say he is the husband in a marriage. His pay-off is that he is able to avoid adult responsibilities. His wife is also an active player in the game. She takes up the parent and saviour role. Her pay-off is that she is able to feel powerful, needed and in control. If she has rather fragile self-esteem this will be immensely valuable to her.

To maintain the game, the child has to drink to excess. He is looked after and protected by the parent. At some point his drinking will get to such a state that he starts to become ill or some other serious consequence occurs. At this point the parent jumps in as saviour, arranging treatment and/or other help for him on an immediate basis. Any attempt to defer this or to make the 'alcoholic' person take responsibility for his own behaviour and treatment will be met with a ferociously protective response. 'How can you be so cruel? This poor man needs help immediately, just look at him, he is a wreck.'

Once saved in this way, the child will accept a metaphorical slapped wrist, something like 'Look at what you've done to me and the family. You've put me under terrible strain. The doctor says I may have an ulcer on the way. It's all your fault.' The child must accept this meekly. He will then go through treatment obediently, without giving the impression that he is very committed. After discharge from the unit he will be good for some time, and will receive a pat on the head from the parent for his efforts at abstinence. However, she will firmly retain control, only allowing him pocket money, insufficient for a bottle of Scotch and putting a lock on the drinks cabinet.

This will continue until a point is reached when, having been sober for some time, the child is at risk of being seen to be able to take on adult responsibilities. There is no longer any reason not to. The parent can see her role disappearing. Both view the impending change as a threat. The odd bottle is inadvertently left open on the sideboard. 'Well, maybe just the one drink, to celebrate our anniversary.'

So the drinking restarts and the roles are confirmed. It continues until the next crisis occurs, when the saviour steps in again. And so on and so on. I have seen this circle lapped some eight times by one couple and I know that this is far from being a record.

This is a game that can clearly have fatal consequences. However, to every game, according to Berne, there is an antithesis – that is, a manoeuvre that stops the game from continuing. One is for the treatment agencies to refuse to respond to the saviour's demands, but to respond only to the child/patient's responsible approaches for treatment. While this is valid, I get the impression that Berne, like me, had considerable difficulties in dealing with the saviour's ferocious defence of the status quo. This approach requires a good lawyer.

I think that in time most people can be persuaded to give up the game, once they have been shown that it is happening and have been helped to achieve their legitimate needs in other ways. The former child has a real difficulty in dealing with responsibility, and to expect him to take a full adult role without time, support and a great deal of counselling would be naive. Equally, the parent is being asked to relinquish possibly her only basis for self-worth, and she will need a lot of understanding of her difficulties in adjusting to the new state of affairs. The fact is, though, that during her period of looking after her alcoholic spouse she will have picked up a number of skills and insights which can be of use to herself and others. These can be used to gain satisfaction in other ways. There is no doubt, though, that she, like any of us, will find it very difficult to stand back if her husband relapses into drinking again in the future. This concept of 'tough love' is espoused by Alcoholics Anonymous and its counterpart, Al-Anon, which I will mention later. She should seek support from people who have gone through it before, and she can find it from Al-Anon. Though Berne felt that these organizations were often involved in the Alcoholic Game, in my view they more often help people out of it.

OK-ness

This seemingly simple concept also comes from Transactional Analysis theory. It is surprisingly often missed, especially by driving, ambitious people. The principle is that it is crucial to be able to see yourself as 'OK' as a person, whatever the ups and downs of your life may do to you. Failure to have this view of yourself firmly embedded may lead to depression, problem drinking or a number of other unpleasant consequences, and it is not possible to enjoy good relationships unless you see both yourself and others as OK.

Managing this will in part depend on your ability to set yourself realistic objectives in your life that allow you not only maximum fulfilment, but can also be maintained for as long as necessary. A term from another branch of psychology that is useful here is 'cognitive dissonance'. This describes what happens when a person holds an ideal view of himself that is unrealistic and unattainable. He will never achieve happiness or fulfilment because he will never reach his image of what he ought to be.

Figure 4.6 Cognitive dissonance

A person without OK-ness will depend a lot on others' approval; he will only feel as good as the last thing someone said to or about him. If he is praised he will feel great, but if criticized he will be totally deflated and lose all self-confidence. He is a cork on the ocean, being buffeted up and down by people's comments and actions.

To illustrate. I know, and will admit publicly here, that I am not the best psychiatrist in the world. There are a couple that I know of who have brains the size of planets, are sensitive, empathic, wonderful human beings, and have a golf handicap of one. People like that make me sick. None the less, I can live with this, because I also know that I am a long way from being the worst. I do as good a job as I can, and that isn't at all bad, though there are areas that could be improved, as with anyone in any job. I'm 'OK' as a psychiatrist. That is enough. This realization is of immense value to me because it allows me to get on with my work without striving to be something that I'm not. I can maximize my potential, have the satisfaction of achieving the goals that I have set myself in my life, and maybe live a bit too.

From time to time, though thankfully rarely, a patient will say to me, 'You have done me no good at all, you are a total waste of time. Why don't you just go away and stop messing me around.' While such a verbal assault is upsetting and makes me think about what has gone wrong, after a while I get it in perspective and it doesn't essentially alter the way I view myself. Occasionally a patient says, 'You are marvellous, you've done wonders for me. You are the best psychiatrist ever.' While I encourage any form of flattery towards me and it is very nice, it doesn't essentially change anything, as by now I have roughly evaluated myself as 'OK'.

When I worked in the academic department of a big London teaching hospital, I had a decision to make. Do I pull out all the stops and try to become Professor of the department, or do I take a straightforward clinical post which I know I can do well. After some agonizing, I chose the latter course and I have never regretted it one bit. I look at some of my contemporaries now, still on the academic treadmill. They have had a lot of trips to exotic parts of the world, delivering important academic papers, but they constantly look worried. Several of them have stomach ulcers. I get the feeling that some of them will view their working lives as a failure unless they achieve the ultimate pinnacle. They are not happy men and women. In any case, whatever they do achieve they tend to discount. They remind me of the Groucho Marx comment: 'I wouldn't want to be a member of a club that would have me as a member'. Before I risk being ostracized by my academic colleagues, let me add that there are many who are well balanced and pursuing fulfilling careers for the healthiest of motives, but the point remains. There must be more to life than a constant struggle against your limitations. There is, but you need to possess a sense of OK-ness to enjoy it.

How do you get this? Try talking to others to find out how they see you. Do some introspection. What do you want to do with your life, in each area of it? Can you achieve this and maintain it for as long as needed, while not robbing other areas of your life that are equally important? If not, maybe it is worth looking for other, more realistic goals. Finally, give yourself credit if you can for what you are and have done, not against the benchmark of your equivalent of the Professor, but against what could reasonably be expected from someone with your abilities and opportunities. You may have your own ideas on this. It's worth giving it some thought.

Family systems theory

This is again a weighty set of theories of vast importance to psychology and psychiatry and I will only touch the very edge of them here.

Systems theory sees people as existing and functioning not as individuals in isolation, but as part of an interconnecting network, within their own family, social group or in society as a whole. That sounds terribly dry, but when you think of it, you don't *behave* at all, except in doing what you are doing, unless there are other people to whom to behave, whether nicely, or nastily, warmly, lovingly or whatever. Whether we like it or not we are part of several systems. How we act and how the system reacts depend on each other.

One important system in our lives is our family. I'll create a hypothetical family here. The individuals in it and their relationships to one another are represented in Figure 4.6 (page 44).

This family has problems. The lines on the diagram denote the family members' strength of attachment to one another and their positions of emotional closeness or distance.

As you can see, the mother is extremely close and attached to her daughter and vice versa, to the exclusion of everyone else. This phenomenon is known as 'enmeshment' and causes difficulties for the whole family. Son 1 tries to get to his mother, but is effectively excluded. Father has long since emotionally turned his back on the family and is separate and aloof from it.

By any standards this is an unsatisfactory set-up, and eventually it will become so clear that it will be commented upon. Confrontation with the awful truth that things are not right and need addressing is painful. If it is brought out into the open and discussed, mutual

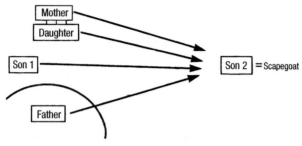

Figure 4.7 A dysfunctional family system

recriminations will follow and that will be even worse. The family needs a smokescreen. To their relief this is provided by Son 2, who has developed a drink problem. Now the rest of the family are safely able to deny their problems, point in unison at him, and say, 'It is all his fault. We haven't got a problem, it's all him.'

Son 2 is performing the valuable role of family scapegoat. They need him, though they aren't aware of it and they honestly believe that he is the problem.

What if Son 2 gets treatment and stops drinking? The whole system is sent into turmoil, and conflict may break out. It is only natural that his efforts will be sabotaged, not consciously or purposely, because in their hearts they care about him, but their unconscious instinct for self-preservation will lead them to disrupt his sobriety. They need their smokescreen/scapegoat back.

It is this sort of situation that sometimes leads to disillusionment and relapse in people recovering from alcoholism. Many people are lucky enough to receive wholehearted support during their recovery, but I warn my patients not to take it for granted.

The essential message here appears to be that during recovery from alcoholism you need to concentrate on yourself and your sobriety above all else. That is your responsibility; other people's difficulties are theirs. Having said this, sympathetic understanding that your new-found sobriety may raise issues that cause your family difficulties is helpful; but returning to drinking is going to help nobody in the long run. Family meetings with a therapist may help, and most drug and alcohol treatment services provide this facility.

Personality research

A lot of work has been done looking for ways in which people who have alcohol problems, or have had them, differ from the rest of the population. The short answer to this is that everyone is different and anyone can develop a drink problem, by just drinking enough for long enough or at the wrong times. There are no personality traits that are possessed by every person suffering a drink problem, or only by them.

Having said this, if large numbers of problem drinkers are compared with corresponding numbers of normal drinkers, some differences emerge between the groups. Four traits are found more often in the alcoholic group.

First, a tendency to impulsiveness. Such a person will drink first or act first and think of the consequences later. Second, rebelliousness. A tendency to oppose and fight against good advice or any rules or imposed regime can cause problems in treatment. Those of us involved in this area of work can sometimes be given quite a rough ride. It is not clear exactly how this is linked to drinking and whether it is cause or effect. It may be that most of us are prevented from acting in ways viewed as socially unacceptable by the fear of condemnation or rejection by society and our peers. If this inhibition is lacking, one could see how a person may drink despite recognizing that his behaviour degenerates when under the influence. Work on resisting impulses, and practice at conforming, can sometimes be important parts of recovery from alcoholism.

The third trait found is called 'the external locus of control'. This refers to a person's feeling that things happen to him rather than him making things happen. He has no control over his life. It all depends on others. This is the 'cork on the ocean' referred to earlier. He is buffeted by the ups and downs that assail him. He takes up a passive role, waiting for the next disaster to befall him, and feels unable to take charge or responsibility for himself. He looks at others and at the world generally with a jaundiced eye and blames 'them', whoever they may be (government, the tax man, the police, traffic wardens, social workers, doctors and spouse are favourite targets), for his misfortunes. In treatment he will need a lot of help with taking control of and responsibility for his life. This can be a long and difficult process as it is much more difficult and emotionally risky to be an actor than a critic.

The final trait found is 'stimulus augmentation'. This works in two ways. Problem drinkers will tend to rate any standard stimulus as greater than will a normal drinker. For example, an injection, rated for painfulness on a scale of 0–10, will tend to be given a higher score by the drinker. At the same time a drinker will tend to try to maximize the sensation she is feeling. If she is feeling bad – perhaps because she has made a mistake at work – she may get drunk. 'I might just as well make a total mess of the whole thing. It's pretty bad anyway, I might as well go the whole hog.' As a result, she makes some more serious mistakes and what should have been a minor inconvenience becomes a major disciplinary matter.

At the other extreme, a drinker will tend to want to make a good feeling great. It would feel almost impossible for such a person just to feel quite good – say, because she had a promotion at work. She would have to put the icing on the cake, probably by 'celebrating with a few drinks'. Many of my patients have told me that the most difficult times to resist the temptation to have a drink are not when they are stressed or when things have gone badly, but when they are feeling happy because they have achieved something. Having a drink to celebrate being a month on the wagon is a well-known route to relapse. Again, getting used to tolerating feelings that are less than extreme will take some practice.

Incidentally, personality studies of illicit drug users tend to show up even fewer patterns. We tend to assume that all drug users conform to the stereotype of the broken-down junkie, unprincipled, unemployed, impulsive and manipulative. In fact, only a minority are like this. We haven't had any royalty through our addictions service yet, but we have had virtually everyone else: doctors, lawyers, policemen, bus-drivers, nurses, academics; they are all represented.

Another popular misconception is that you can't change your personality. You can; and what is more, your personality changes through your life whether you like it or not. Personality, after all, can only be defined by how you behave. It is not a static thing, but fluid, changing minutely as a result of every experience and action. I am certainly a very different person than I was ten years ago.

The way to go about changing your personality is to *act that way*. For example, if you are an introvert and you want to become more gregarious and extraverted, you can do it by behaving as if you were an extravert – going to parties, seeking group activities, talking to lots of new people, etc. This will seem very difficult, odd and false at first, but in time you will actually become that way.

The most spectacular example of this phenomenon that I know of is the two American psychologists who got themselves admitted to separate psychiatric hospitals as part of an experiment. They planned to simulate schizophrenia so that the staff would be unaware that they were actually observing the workings of the hospital system from within. The plan was that they would both stop their roles after six months, reveal their real identities, and present their findings. The trouble was that when the six months were up they were both genuinely disturbed, apparently suffering from schizophrenia. To my knowledge, they remain affected to this day.

So you can change your personality by concerted action. It may be necessary to do so if your personality has made a major contribution to your drinking. More of this in a later chapter.

Part 3
WHAT'S THE HARM IN HEAVY DRINKING?

5

Effects of alcohol abuse on the liver

This chapter is quite alarming. It is not my intention to frighten or intimidate. You may be thinking, 'He's doing a scare job here because he thinks that will stop people drinking.' That isn't my style. After all, if I were to exaggerate I would soon be contradicted and no one would believe me any more. On the other hand, I won't pull any punches either, because I believe that everyone deserves to be well informed, particularly about something as dangerous as drinking too much. What follows is as objective as I can make it. Let me stress again, though, that if you drink moderately you are probably in greater danger of being run over by a bus than you are of coming to physical harm from your drinking.

The liver

In its normal state the liver sits underneath the ribcage on the right side of the body. It is separated from the lungs by a sheet of muscle called the diaphragm. One of its main functions is to break down substances absorbed in the bloodstream into harmless molecules that can be excreted, usually through the kidneys. This process is called metabolism. In particular, drugs such as alcohol are metabolized by the liver. This is done by chemicals in the liver cells called enzymes.

Alcohol is unusual in that the rate at which it is metabolized is independent of the amount in the body. Whether you have drunk 1 pint of beer or 10 pints, you will get rid of it at the rate of about 1 unit (half a pint of regular strength (3.8% abv) beer) an hour. Regular heavy drinkers may break it down rather faster than this. This is why, if you have a heavy drinking session in the evening, you may well still be over the legal limit for driving the next morning. Assuming the legal limit is reached with about 2½ pints of regular-strength beer in men (1½ pints in women), that you are male, of average weight with average metabolism, that you drank quite quickly over a short period and that you are on the road seven hours after you finished drinking, you will still be over the limit if you drank over 6 pints in the session. That is, you will have metabolized 3½ pints (7 units) during the night. Beware of interpreting this rule too literally, as everyone's rate of metabolism is a bit different.

Alcohol is toxic. In large quantities it damages the liver cells that are metabolizing it. In the early stages the cells become inflamed. With continued exposure cells begin to die, and when this happens they burst.

If you have been drinking too much, your doctor may take a blood test. One of the things looked for in this test is the level of the liver's enzymes in the bloodstream. There are several of these, and I will mention three of them here as you may want to look at your own blood test result and draw some conclusions from it. These three are the Gamma GT, AST and ALT. Their normal levels in the bloodstream are given in Table 5.1 (some laboratories use different scales, but normal ranges are usually printed on the result form). These levels reflect that even in the absence of any damage from alcohol or anything else, liver cells die off at a slow rate, releasing their enzymes into the blood. Fortunately, we have plenty of liver cells – far more than we need to last a lifetime, and cells that are lost are continually replaced, so this background slow loss of cells doesn't matter. But if you are drinking to excess, the accelerated rate of liver cell death may be very serious. In excessive drinking, the Gamma GT tends to be the first to rise, maybe because it can leak out of liver cells that are still alive but inflamed. For example, if as a usually moderate drinker I drink 6 pints of beer or two bottles of wine at a party today, my Gamma GT may well be about 70 if measured tomorrow. The AST and ALT need much more prolonged excessive drinking to be raised and don't usually go so high, maybe because only dead liver cells that have burst will release these enzymes. I have seen Gamma GT levels over 2,000, whereas an ALT of 70 is seriously raised. By contrast, the Gamma GT often comes down quickly (days usually), whereas the AST and ALT sometimes take much longer (weeks).

Table 5.1 Liver enzymes

Enzyme	Normal level below
Gamma GT	50
ALT	40
AST	40

Note: These figures vary slightly from one laboratory to another.

The reason why I have taken you through this bit of biochemistry is because by looking at your result you can gain a fair impression of what is going on in your liver, and that may give you an idea as to how urgently you need to address your drinking.

The other test that is often done is the full blood count. Two figures on this are of particular interest. Their normal ranges are given in Table 5.2.

Table 5.2 Full blood count ranges

Parameter	Normal range
MCV	85–98 (approx.)
Platelets	150–400

MCV stands for Mean Cellular Volume, or the size of your red blood cells. These are the cells in your blood that carry oxygen around your body. They are made in the marrow in the middle of your bones and need a well-functioning liver and a supply of Vitamin B12 to be properly made. But apart from damaging the liver, alcohol stops Vitamin B12 from being fully absorbed by the body. The bone marrow will therefore be under pressure in a heavy drinker. Like any production line, if the marrow is under too much pressure it will turn out a half-made product. Immature red blood cells are swollen and ball-shaped, only later shrinking into a small concave plate shape that is perfect for carrying oxygen.

The presence of enlarged red cells in the blood as shown by a raised MCV means that your drinking is affecting your liver and stopping Vitamin B12 being absorbed, so stopping your bone marrow from working properly.

Platelets, also made by the bone marrow, need a healthy liver and won't be made in sufficient numbers if your liver is suffering damage. These small sticky fragments are essential for blood clotting. If you cut yourself, two things happen within minutes. First, a network of sticky strands too small to see are laid down at the site of the cut. Second, the platelets get stuck in this network, forming a plug. This is what forms the clot that stops the bleeding. Without platelets, you would go on bleeding from the cut indefinitely. We get worried if the platelet count falls to around 50, because at around this level clots do not form properly and bleeding may occur without any significant injury. A transfusion or medication may be required. We therefore keep a close eye on this figure in heavy drinkers.

One more blood test looking at the blood's clotting system is also sometimes done when we are concerned about the health of your liver. This is the prothrombin time (nowadays usually called INR), which is a measure of how long it takes the blood to clot in particular circumstances. This clotting takes longer when the liver is failing to work properly, so the test gives us an early warning sign of this potentially dangerous situation.

You may want to have a look at your blood test results to check on these things. Your doctor will probably be happy for you to do so, if asked, and to give advice on anything that needs clarification.

What happens in liver damage

Though liver cells regenerate, with excessive alcohol consumption the rate of liver cell death exceeds the rate at which new cells are made. The dead cells at first get replaced by fat and later by scar tissue.

As I have said before, there are plenty of liver cells in reserve under normal circumstances. However, if by drinking too much you accelerate the rate of liver cell death, you eventually won't have enough to survive. It varies from person to person, but say we need about 30 per cent of our liver cells to be working for it to function. The actual percentage isn't known, but this isn't far wrong. This is the limitation of gauging liver function through the level of liver enzymes in the blood. The latter tells us the rate at which liver cells are dying, whereas what we would really like to know is what proportion are left and how much scar tissue is present. This scarring makes it much more difficult for remaining liver cells to function and limits the ability of the liver to regenerate effectively. Unfortunately, the only way of finding this out is through a liver biopsy in which a small piece of liver is extracted and viewed under a microscope. As this procedure isn't very pleasant it is not carried out routinely.

The liver is a robust organ. It continues to function perfectly well even when quite a lot of its cells have died. In fact if anything, its

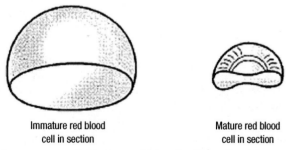

Immature red blood   Mature red blood
cell in section   cell in section

Figure 5.1 Immature and mature red blood cells

effectiveness at metabolizing the drug (in this case alcohol) that has damaged it increases. Most regular drinkers recognize that it takes a lot more to get tipsy now than it used to when they first started drinking. That is because the liver is metabolizing alcohol more quickly (an effect called tolerance). There is a limit to this increased effectiveness, as you can see from Figure 5.1.

As more and more cells die, the liver continues to function well. It is rather like a factory in which workers are being laid off. As workers are lost, the rest have to work harder, and the increased efficiency causes productivity that is as good or better than before. Another worker lost puts the system under strain, but everyone copes, just, and no harm can be detected in the product. But just one more lay-off is the straw that breaks the camel's back and the whole production line collapses all of a sudden (see Figure 5.2).

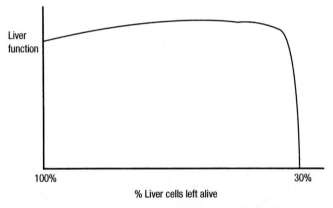

Figure 5.2 **Liver function versus percentage functioning cells**

This is what happens to the liver at a predetermined proportion of cells lost – say, around 70 per cent – though, as mentioned earlier, this varies from person to person and depends on the amount of scar tissue present. From working well, its demise is sudden in many cases. You may get little or no warning of liver failure. While some people survive even after symptoms of liver failure have occurred, they do not do so for long if they continue drinking, and some people die quite suddenly at this point.

Having said this, there are a few physical signs that suggest that alcohol is beginning to harm your liver without being an indication of imminent liver failure. We all recognize the 'drinker's nose'. The red, bloodshot appearance of the cheeks, and especially the nose, is partly a reflection of the fact that alcohol dilates blood vessels and partly due to the opening up of new vessels, which occurs when the liver is under strain. These new vessels have a characteristic appearance and are called 'Spider Naevi' – or 'spiders' for short (see Figure 5.3).

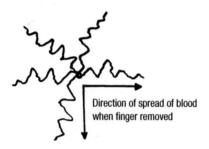

Direction of spread of blood
when finger removed

Figure 5.3 A spider naevus

They are small, with a central point and tiny arms radiating out, making them look like a money spider. You can tell them from other small capillaries (very small blood vessels) by the fact that if you press one and then release, you will see it fill up from the centre outwards.

Received wisdom has it that it is normal to have up to three spider naevi on your body, commonly on the face or upper chest. Many more than this may reflect liver disease. There are some exceptions to this rule. For example, it is normal to have more than three spider naevi in pregnancy.

Another early sign of problems is the appearance of 'liver palms'. This is a bright red appearance around the fleshy base of the thumb and around the base of the palm of the hand. Usually at a later stage, a deformity of the hand called 'Dupuytren's Contracture' may occur (see Figure 5.4). The little, middle and ring fingers on either hand curl up and cannot be held straight out.

The most obvious but least visible sign is an enlarged liver. Under normal circumstances the liver cannot be felt because it is hidden underneath the ribcage on the right side of your body. In order for it to be felt below the ribcage, it has to be enlarged to about three times its original volume. Your doctor will feel for your liver by pressing into your abdomen on the right just below your ribcage and asking you to take a deep breath in. If it is greatly enlarged, he/she will feel it as you breathe in. Beware of self-diagnosis here; it is easy to alarm yourself unnecessarily by mistaking a rib for the edge of your liver.

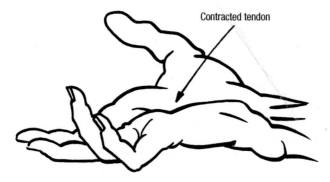

Contracted tendon

Figure 5.4 Dupuytren's Contracture

The liver enlarges in excessive drinking because as liver cells die they are replaced first by fat, which takes up a lot of space, then by scar tissue. You will know that if you cut yourself and are left with a scar, it stands proud of the surrounding skin. This is because scar tissue takes up a greater volume than the tissue that it replaces. The same is true for the liver. As cells are killed by alcohol, the scar tissue takes up a bigger volume and so the liver grows in size.

If any of these earlier signs of liver strain have appeared on your body, it is time to stop drinking and get medical help, because if you continue drinking you will sooner or later die from total liver failure. Another risk if you continue drinking is of liver cancer.

Death from liver failure can come about in one of three ways. First, by poisoning. The liver metabolizes most things that we take into our bodies, many of which would otherwise be poisonous. When the liver fails and poisoning follows, the affected person may or may not develop a yellow tint rather like a fading suntan (jaundice), will become muddled, clumsy and drowsy, may show a flapping tremor of the hands, and will eventually lapse into a coma and then die.

The second cause is oedema – that is, the collection of fluid in the body. The liver makes the small proteins that are the osmotic components of the blood. Osmosis is the process that you see if you watch what happens when some spilt tea meets a mound of spilt sugar. The tea is suddenly sucked into the sugar by osmosis. The small proteins do this for the blood, which is just as well as the blood is mostly water and without them this water would leak out of the blood vessels; these are far from impermeable, because they need to be able to let oxygen and nutrients pass through to get to the parts of the body for which they are destined. Without these proteins, fluid leaks from the blood into anywhere that it can. The ankles, being at the lowest point of the body, where the pressure of blood pushing down is greatest, are the first to develop this oedema. In fact, many people, especially pregnant women and older people, may sometimes get oedema of the ankles after standing for a long time, and in these circumstances it is not an indication of liver disease. You can tell oedema from any other swelling because if you press it in with your thumb it will leave an indentation when your thumb is removed.

Oedema fluid may also collect in the abdomen, causing great swelling, sometimes making the person look pregnant. Most seriously, the fluid may collect in the lungs, gradually filling them up so that the person can no longer breathe.

The third cause is the formation of 'oesophageal varices'. When the liver has been filled up with a lot of scar tissue, a point comes, often suddenly, when the remaining liver cells can no longer support themselves, and are crushed by the scar. You will have noticed how a large scar on your skin will eventually contract, causing the skin around it to become puckered. If there aren't enough liver cells to prevent it, this happens in the liver and, from being enlarged, it rapidly shrinks to a solid mass about the size of a large grapefruit and as solid as a rock. Blood vessels pass from the whole of the gut to the liver and the most delicate of these come from the oesophagus (the tube from your mouth to your stomach). These are normally small vessels, but when the liver shrinks, the blood cannot get through it and a massive back pressure develops, causing these veins to become greatly distended, sometimes becoming bigger than the oesophagus itself. They press on the oesophagus and eventually erode into it. When this occurs, the haemorrhage may be anything from a few drops to a torrent that leads to a loss of virtually the total blood volume in a matter of minutes.

This is all rather grim, but the truth is that liver failure is not a nice way to go and I believe that anyone who is taking the risk of developing it has the right to know what can happen. I am afraid that this is far from being all the damage that alcohol can do to the body either.

6

The effect of alcohol on other parts of the body

As you will see in this chapter, alcohol is a remarkable drug. It affects the parts that other drugs cannot reach. The human body has an awful lot of bits in it and alcohol in excess can harm almost all of them (see Figure 6.1).

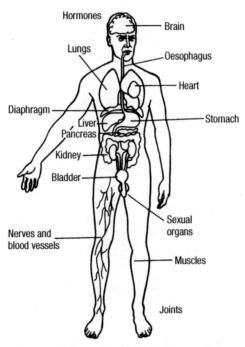

Figure 6.1 The human body with organs affected by excessive drinking

The stomach

Alcohol is very caustic. You will find it in many industrial solvents, and all party hosts know that spilling booze on the carpet and forgetting to wash it off leads to serious damage. The stomach isn't immune from this, though it is a pretty hardy organ. Alcohol in excess causes it to become inflamed, especially if it isn't accompanied by food. Most excessive drinkers don't eat properly, and so the stomach often gets chronically inflamed. Any area where this is particularly bad may become eroded and form an ulcer; that is, an area where the stomach lining has worn through, exposing nerve endings and blood vessels. This may be painful and it may bleed. If the person vomits, the blood will look brown in colour, often like coffee grounds, because of the effect of stomach acid on the blood. The effect of this acid on the eroded stomach wall makes the inflammation even worse. The most common location for an ulcer caused by drinking is directly below the opening of the oesophagus, which is not surprising as this is where the alcohol you drink first strikes the stomach (presuming you drink in an upright position). If erosion of an ulcer continues, it can eventually punch a hole right through.

What happens then is very unpleasant. This is because of the nature of the peritoneum, which is the skin-like covering of the gut (see Figure 6.2).

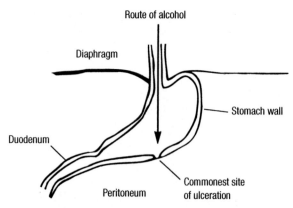

Figure 6.2 Alcohol on the stomach

The peritoneum is packed full of nerve endings and so is extremely sensitive; much more so than the skin. When a stomach ulcer perforates, alcohol, food and, worst of all, stomach acid leak out into the peritoneum. Stomach acid is powerful stuff and this will be exceptionally painful. In fact, the major risk to life at this time is a fall in blood pressure caused by shock due to the severity of the pain.

This is a medical emergency and requires urgent hospital treatment. Providing this is given quickly, the vast majority of people nowadays survive this crisis.

The pancreas

This organ has two main functions. The first is to produce insulin, the hormone that is lacking in diabetics. Not surprisingly, alcohol damage to the pancreas makes established diabetes worse and can cause diabetes in some people who didn't previously suffer from it (Type 2 diabetes).

The second is to produce the pancreatic juice, which is released into the first part of the intestine, the duodenum, in response to food (see Figure 6.3).

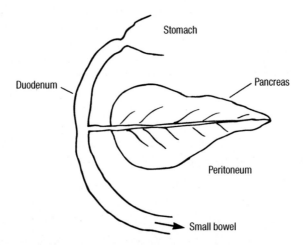

Figure 6.3 The pancreas and duodenum

Pancreatic juice is tremendous stuff. It never ceases to amaze me how the body manages to take virtually anything you shove into it at one end and by the time the remains come out at the other end all that is left is a soft mush. It must take something pretty special to do that to anything from a full English breakfast to an apple. That something special is primarily the pancreatic juice, though there are other digestive juices further down the intestine which help the process along. It is also a great wonder to my mind that the duodenum is able to cope with this exceptionally caustic substance. It does this by being covered by a protective layer which prevents it being burnt away. All is well if the juice only enters the duodenum. However, excessive drinking can lead to inflammation of the pancreas, pancreatitis. This causes the pancreas to become leaky. The pancreatic juice then leaks out into the delicate and super-sensitive peritoneum. The result is along the same lines as in perforation of a stomach ulcer (above), but owing to the extremely caustic nature of pancreatic juice, symptoms may be even more severe.

In both pancreatitis and perforation of a stomach ulcer the crucial thing is to prevent a tragedy by getting to hospital quickly. This doesn't mean rushing down to Casualty every time you get a stomach ache. The pain from perforation or pancreatitis is unmistakable and will be many times more severe than anything you have experienced before. If such an agonizing pain in the abdomen does occur, however, particularly if it comes on quite suddenly and you are a heavy drinker, you must get medical attention quickly.

As a doctor working in the field of problem drinking, I am well aware that whatever is done in treatment, many people relapse one or more times before they finally beat the problem. One of my priorities, therefore, is to keep people alive so that they are around to have another go at treatment. These two complications are examples of how prompt recognition and action can allow this to happen.

Kidneys

Drinking excessively causes an excess of uric acid to be excreted and sometimes to accumulate in the kidney (see Figure 6.4).

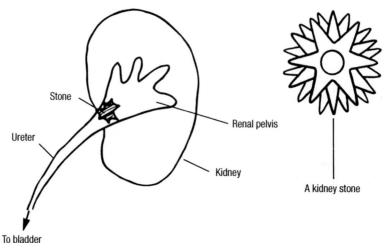

Figure 6.4 The kidney with stone

When this substance hangs around in sufficient quantities for long enough, it forms into crystals and even into a stone. This stone will be sharp and spiky and may be too big to fit in the ureter (the tube emptying out from the kidney to the bladder). It will therefore stay put and may seriously damage the ureter and kidney. This condition is usually very painful and may be accompanied by a loss of blood into the urine, making the urine pink or red in colour. The pain is usually in one flank and, unlike the pain of peritonitis from a perforated stomach ulcer or pancreatitis, it is usually colicky. That is, it tends to come and go in waves every few minutes. This corresponds to the periodic efforts of the ureter to push the sharp object down towards the bladder.

Joints

Uric acid, produced in excess through heavy drinking, does not only collect in the kidneys. It will also tend to accumulate in the joints, particularly the smaller ones. Crystals form, and in the small space available these tend to be small sharp splinters, rather like splinters of broken glass. The most commonly affected joint is that between the foot and the big toe. It becomes red, swollen and exquisitely tender to the touch, so much so that even the weight of a sheet on it can be very painful. This is gout, the affliction of wine drinkers through the ages, though alcohol taken to excess in any form can cause it (see Figure 6.5).

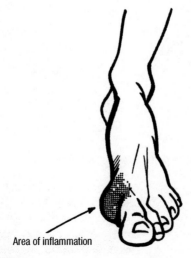

Area of inflammation

Figure 6.5 A gouty joint

Nerves

Alcohol is toxic to nerve fibres. Nerves are the electrical cables that transmit messages throughout the body to and from the brain. There are three main types: motor nerves, which lead to the muscles, allowing movement to occur; sensory nerves, which lead from all parts of the body, producing feelings, including touch and pain; and autonomic nerves, which control the function of parts of the body that are not under conscious control, such as the heart and the bowels.

The nerves most vulnerable to attack from excess alcohol are the longest ones, especially those to the feet and legs. Damage to the motor nerves contributes to difficulty in walking, while sensory-nerve damage causes pins and needles, pain and, conversely, sometimes numbness in the feet. As the condition progresses, this numbness spreads further up the leg. The hands can also be affected, leading to the term 'glove and stocking anaesthesia' where numbness has occurred (see Figure 6.6).

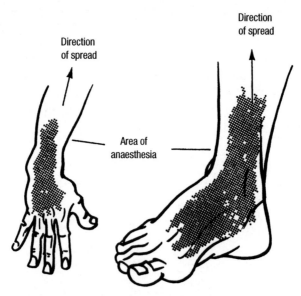

Figure 6.6 Glove and stocking anaesthesia

This is potentially very damaging as without feeling in the feet it is difficult to know where or what you are stepping on, and severe damage to the feet can result. We don't think of pain as being a good thing, but it is very necessary as a warning of damage to the body, and without it you would, for example, fail to remove your hand from a hot ring on a cooker until you smelt the burning, by which time skin grafting might be required. The risk of this complication is particularly high in people who have or develop diabetes.

Long nerve damage is also partly caused by lack of Vitamin B1, thiamine. This vitamin is essential to proper functioning of the long nerves. It is often lacking in heavy drinkers, partly due to the fact that as drinking progresses, appetite is lost, so causing inadequate intake of thiamine; and partly because alcohol inhibits the uptake of this vitamin into the body. It is true that improving diet or taking thiamine supplements can to some extent protect against this complication, but alcohol inhibits its absorption, and so limits the effectiveness of this safeguard in very heavy drinkers. This is why high-potency vitamins are sometimes given by injection in alcohol treatment units, despite the discomfort that this entails.

Damage to autonomic nerves may have a number of harmful effects around the body. Notable among these are that it can cause failure to achieve erection in men and inability to experience orgasm in women.

Muscles

Excessive drinking can cause inflammation of muscles, particularly in the legs and (see later) the heart. It is ironic that while the feet may be numb, the muscles above them may be very tender and painful. This pain tends to be worse after a binge. If drinking continues, this can lead to permanent damage to these muscles, leaving them flabby and weak. This may be another contributory factor to the problem drinker's difficulty in walking.

Hormones

Several hormone systems can be affected by alcohol, but the most noticeable can be those controlling sexual characteristics. Women may grow hair on the face and elsewhere and become more masculine in appearance. They may lose their menstrual periods and become unable to conceive. Beware, though; alcohol even in vast amounts is not a reliable contraceptive. If a women suffering loss of fertility from excessive drinking stops or cuts down to normal levels, her fertility will often return, but this cannot be relied upon. In rare cases sterility may be permanent.

Correspondingly, men may lose facial hair, grow breasts and suffer shrinkage of their testicles, with the same risk of infertility (see Figure 6.7).

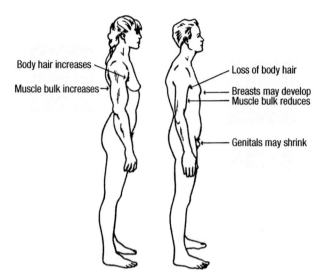

Body hair increases

Muscle bulk increases

Loss of body hair

Breasts may develop
Muscle bulk reduces

Genitals may shrink

Figure 6.7 Altered sexual characteristics

Heart

The heart is composed almost entirely of muscle. As already mentioned, excessive drinking damages muscle, and the heart is not immune from this. The condition is known as 'alcoholic cardiomyopathy', which means weakness of the heart muscle due to drinking. The heart becomes flabby and ineffective at pumping blood around the body. As in the late stages of liver disease, fluid may accumulate in the lungs. The sufferer will become increasingly weak and breathless and may eventually become unable to lie flat without being short of breath. Sadly, by this stage the heart is irreparably damaged, though drugs such as diuretics (water tablets) may lessen the breathlessness.

Blood vessels

Alcohol causes the capillaries in the skin to open up. This causes the flushing of the face when you have had a drink, the 'warm glow' that is supposed to keep out the cold. In fact, the opposite is true. The loss of heat from these dilated blood vessels will cool you down. If you are ever unfortunate enough to be buried in an avalanche, I hope that your luck changes sufficiently for you to be dug out by a friendly St Bernard. But whatever you do, don't take a drink from the barrel around its neck. The loss of heat from dilation of your capillaries could kill you.

In regular heavy drinkers this dilation of the capillaries becomes permanent. This is the cause of the 'drinker's nose' and the reason why the man who is always at the bar when you go in and still there when you leave has such a ruddy complexion (see Figure 6.8).

Figure 6.8 A drinker's face

Cancer

Cancer is much more common in excessive drinkers than in the rest of the population. Particularly common are cancer of the liver, bladder or lung. The last of these is partly accounted for by the fact that many heavy drinkers also smoke heavily. The link between lung cancer and smoking is, of course, well known. But this is not the whole story; even non-smoking problem drinkers are at increased risk.

Alcohol in pregnancy

Alcohol, like many drugs, crosses the placenta, the attachment of the umbilical cord between the mother and her baby in the womb. Every drink you take is also taken by the foetus. The usual advice given to pregnant mothers is not to drink alcohol at all during pregnancy, though a very occasional drink probably does no harm.

It isn't quite clear what the safe level of drinking is in pregnancy, but it is certainly less than the 14 units maximum advised at other times.

Having one drink on one occasion is very unlikely to do the baby any harm, but it's probably safer not to drink at all when pregnant.

However, heavy drinking during pregnancy (say over 35 units a week) can sometimes have very serious consequences. The baby may be born with the 'foetal alcohol syndrome'. In this condition the baby has stunted growth, physical disabilities, facial abnormalities and develops poorly intellectually. Fortunately, this fully developed form of the condition is fairly rare, but lesser degrees are probably more common in excessive drinkers. It is certainly worth being particularly careful about drinking during pregnancy – and never to get drunk – though there is no evidence that you need to worry if you have had the odd episode of overindulgence before you realized you were pregnant.

From the above, and Figure 6.1, you will see that there is almost no part of the body that is immune from the harmful effects of excessive drinking. However, we still haven't considered the organ that is most vulnerable of all: the brain.

7

The effect of alcohol on the brain

The brain is a delicate organ and is particularly vulnerable to the effects of excessive drinking. As in the previous chapters, though, you can be reassured that drinking occasionally, within recommended limits, will not lead to the horrors that will be described here.

Pathological intoxication

Drunkenness is such a common phenomenon in Western society that I don't need to describe the dangers of it here; indeed, most people have experienced it at some time in their lives. Suffice it to say that common intoxication with alcohol is one of the major killers in the UK through road and other accidents, and alcohol is involved in the majority of cases of violence and other crime.

Though intoxication from consumption of large amounts of drink is common, there is also a much less common condition in which an individual may become dangerously drunk after drinking only a small amount. Such a person may become suddenly aggressive or violent, or his behaviour may change in an uncharacteristic way after a single drink.

It is not clear just how often this phenomenon occurs, but it turns up not uncommonly in court as a defence to a charge of criminal behaviour. The law does not hold drunkenness as any excuse for crime, because while a drunk person may not know what he is doing and may not mean to act unlawfully, he is deemed as being responsible for getting drunk, knowing that this might rob him of the discretion necessary to avoid falling foul of the law. But if it can be shown that the state of intoxication occurred unexpectedly, on amounts of alcohol that would not normally be expected to cause any problem, the person is held as less responsible than he would have been for his actions. This defence doesn't often work. Juries are not usually composed of fools.

There is no doubt that this phenomenon does occur occasionally, though, and can have very serious and even fatal results. The implication is obvious. If even a small amount of drink changes your behaviour for the worse, it is well worth avoiding the stuff altogether.

Your vulnerability to alcohol will not disappear with age; in fact, it may increase, and so a return to drinking should only be attempted with great caution.

Alcohol withdrawal symptoms

I am often surprised by how much some people can drink without suffering withdrawal symptoms on drink-free days, while others apparently get physically addicted when drinking only a little over the high-risk limit. In my view, though, the latter individuals are the lucky ones, getting an early warning that their drinking is causing them harm. So long as they seek help at this stage, they are likely to escape the worst penalties of alcoholism.

The withdrawal symptoms on suddenly stopping drinking once physically addicted are characteristically: a feeling of anxiety, usually apparent first thing in the morning, accompanied by shakiness and clumsiness and often by general discomfort. Nausea, loss of appetite and retching can also happen. If nothing is done, the symptoms reach a peak at between one and three days and are usually gone within five days to a week. The victim can obtain immediate relief by having a stiff drink. So the dreadful vicious circle is set up of even heavier drinking to keep withdrawal symptoms at bay (see Figure 7.1).

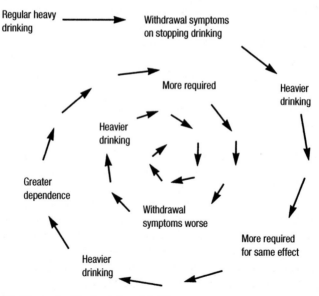

Figure 7.1 The spiral to heavier drinking

Fortunately, help is at hand. Modern tranquillizing drugs, given in tapering dosage over about a week, can more or less obliterate these symptoms. They also greatly reduce the risk of one of the most serious possible withdrawal symptoms – epileptic fits. In severely addicted drinkers, while fits are not the norm, they are not uncommon either and can even very occasionally occur when the person is receiving medical treatment. In my view, if someone is so severely addicted that he gets badly shaky first thing in the morning and has a drink to settle himself down, or if he has a family history or past history of epilepsy, the only safe thing for him to do is to be detoxified (given medication to help him come off alcohol) under close supervision in hospital. Less severely addicted people can safely take the prescribed medication at home, preferably with someone around for the first few days. You mustn't drive or operate potentially dangerous machinery while on this medication. Above all, don't try to stop drinking suddenly if you have suffered any withdrawal symptoms of the type described above, but go to your GP for advice and treatment.

These symptoms are caused by a rebound reversal of the initial effects of alcohol on the brain (see Chapter 2). Occasionally, an even more severe withdrawal reaction can occur – delirium tremens.

Delirium tremens

'The DTs' are commonly thought of as referring to the withdrawal symptoms described above, but in fact the term refers to a much more hazardous occasional complication of withdrawal. Untreated, it is sometimes even fatal.

The first signs are the same as these common withdrawal symptoms. However, the sufferer becomes progressively more frightened and shaky and then starts to become muddled. Typically, a little later he starts to suffer visual hallucinations; that is, he sees things that are not there. He may see spiders crawling over the wall, or the shapes of other animals, or indeed any object at all. He may hear voices or other sounds. Commonly he is terrified by these experiences, though occasionally patients seem to be unmoved or even amused by them.

At this point he will probably start to feel threatened and may feel that the people around him are trying to attack him. He may retaliate in self-defence against this imaginary attack. I once saw a patient who went berserk while in this state and I will never forget either his destructive power or the terror in his eyes.

This is the point at which the person may collapse, and if he is not under medical supervision, he may die. The cause is shock. He dies of fright.

Shock in the medical sense is a condition where the blood pressure falls to a level that is dangerous. It occurs when a lot of blood is lost, or when the blood vessels all open up together to such an extent that the blood within them is insufficient to maintain enough pressure for the blood to get to the brain. The occurrence of this reaction to a sudden alarm is a favourite of Hollywood movies, though I have never understood why it is always the heroine and never the hero who swoons, or how she manages to avoid a head injury by collapsing so gracefully.

Delirium tremens is another of the alcohol-induced conditions that, while a medical emergency, is very easily treated. The trick is having someone around with their wits about them to call a doctor or even an ambulance. An intravenous injection of a tranquillizer followed by a course of detoxification is all that is required. The sufferer will be a lot better within minutes, and as right as rain in a few days.

In my view, anyone who is drinking enough to risk becoming physically addicted to alcohol needs to know about this potential complication and, more particularly, so does anyone living with them, because having this knowledge and acting on it can be the difference between life and death.

Incidentally, what I have described is a typical picture of DTs, but it can take various forms, with some of the symptoms missing or occurring out of sequence. Any state in a heavy drinker entailing extreme fear, a confused or muddled state when not drunk, or hallucinations, needs to be treated with caution.

Wernicke's Encephalopathy and Korsakoff's Psychosis

I don't know about you, but medical terms tend to amuse me. Take Wernicke's Encephalopathy. Not so much a mouthful as a meal in itself. I think that doctors make up these terms as a secret language so that patients can't understand what they are saying and therefore think that they must be very clever. Actually, all it means is a condition described by a man called Wernicke in which the brain (encephal-) doesn't work properly (-opathy). The condition is another of the states caused by too much drinking that constitutes a medical emergency.

This disorder usually occurs in someone who is continuing to drink, though I have seen it crop up by chance in someone who had stopped drinking a few days earlier. Again, there is a typical full-blown form that I will describe, but partial and unusual types can occur.

The first thing that is usually noticed is that the sufferer begins to appear more drunk than would be expected for the amount of drink consumed. He will start to slur, become clumsy, maybe knocking over his glass and bumping into things. As in DTs, he will start to become muddled, but unlike that condition he is not usually frightened. All these symptoms will get progressively worse. Then the unmistakable cardinal symptom occurs. He develops a squint.

It is crucial that at this stage or before he receives medical attention. If he does not, he will eventually sink into unconsciousness.

When he wakes up, which may be minutes, hours or even days later, he will at first sight appear normal. He may say he feels fine. But all is far from well. In the full-blown form he has Korsakoff's Psychosis. This is another long-winded term and is, in fact, a misnomer. A psychosis is a condition in which the sufferer loses touch with reality and may suffer delusions (false beliefs) and hallucinations. These symptoms do not occur here. What does occur is a total inability to set down any new memories, even though old memories remain intact.

This may seem inconvenient, but if you think about the implications you will realize that it is a disaster. If you can't remember what you have just done, why you are where you are, that you turned the gas on but haven't yet lit the flame, or where the shops are, you will be unable to live an independent life. People with the full form of this condition are usually institutionalized for the rest of their lives.

The reason why this may seem to be a psychosis is the phenomenon of confabulation. As the victim has either a blank memory from the time of awakening from coma or at least has big gaps in it, his mind naturally tries to fill the gap so as to make some sense of the world around him. The mind does this in everyone all the time. If while sitting on the loo you look down at the lino on the floor, you will tend not to see just a random set of patterns in the material, but will be able to make out a face here and the shape of an object, person or animal there. Another person will see a completely different set of things in the same random pattern. The mind is imposing a pattern on the meaningless because it is constructed to see things as meaningful wholes and not just a set of parts. A face is not a nose, two eyes, a mouth, ears, cheeks and the rest, but is a face. The same phenomenon is at play in confabulation. The gap in memory is filled with a set of events constructed around the few fragments of real memory that are present. The events are fictitious, but are fully believed by the victim. The bizarre recounting of a visit made yesterday, when the listener knows that the speaker was at home all day, seems like a delusion. Sadly, it is even more serious and permanent than that. To make things worse, the victim often suffers an all-round deterioration in his ability to think as well.

Wernicke's Encephalopathy happens because of a lack of thiamine.

As I have mentioned, this vitamin is stopped from getting into the body by alcohol and is usually not present anyway because of the drinker's loss of interest in food. Without it, the very smallest capillary blood vessels begin to leak, particularly those around a part of the brain on its underside called the hypothalamus (see Figure 7.2).

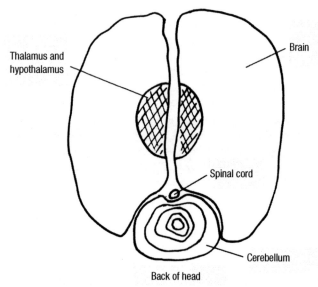

Figure 7.2 The underside of the brain with the hypothalamus

It is this part of the brain that is responsible for the laying down of new memories. It is as if thiamine were acting like a sort of glue between the cells making up the walls of the capillaries. These blood vessels at their smallest are only one cell thick. The more demand a structure in the body has for oxygen and energy, the smaller will be the capillaries in and around it, as the thinner the wall, the easier it is for blood gases and sugars to pass across from the blood to the tissue. The hypothalamus needs a lot of oxygen and energy – memory is a very energetic function – so it has a vast amount of these tiny capillaries.

It is amazing how the blood cells and plasma fluid in the blood don't leak out of these capillaries. Without thiamine, they do. The signs of Wernicke's Encephalopathy occur when the blood is leaking out of the capillaries into and around the hypothalamus. Unconsciousness occurs when so much blood has leaked out that the pressure inside the skull is increased. Like any pool of blood, it eventually clots; and as it does so, it shrinks into a small hard lump. The pressure in the skull falls and so the patient wakes up. Unfortunately, the solid blood clot has by this point damaged the brain tissue around it. Hence the loss of ability to memorize.

As with DTs, the earlier that action is taken in this condition, the better. If the sufferer is given an injection of thiamine intravenously before unconsciousness occurs, he will probably recover fully and be left with no problems with his memory. If he isn't, then it is probably too late. As before, the message is for someone close to you to recognize what is happening and get medical assistance urgently.

Alcoholic dementia

There is a commonly held fallacy that all old people become senile. I am happy to report that this is not true. The vast majority of people can live to a hundred without losing their essential mental faculties. Though we lose brain cells at a steady rate through life, there are plenty enough in reserve to meet the demands put on the brain throughout our lives.

In fact, in senile dementia it isn't actually the increased loss of brain cells that causes the problem, but the effect of the dead cells on the working of the cells that are left alive. Nerve cells, including those in the brain, are essentially electrical cables. In senile dementia (also called Alzheimer's disease) the dead cells form tangles that cause short-circuiting in the cables around them. Information being relayed is therefore jumbled up, causing the brain as a whole to malfunction. Personality changes, intellect wanes, memory deteriorates (particularly memory for recent events) and, in advanced cases, control over bodily functions is lost.

Alzheimer's disease can happen to younger people too, but this is fortunately rare. However, if brain cells die at an accelerated rate for any reason, dementia can occur at a very young age indeed. One such cause is alcohol, and I have witnessed patients suffer this inexorable decline tragically in their forties, following years of excessive drinking. Brain cells, once dead, stay dead and are not replaced. Patients do not recover from alcoholic dementia even if they stop drinking, and there is no cure.

Alcoholic hallucinosis

This is not a life-threatening condition, but it is still a good idea to get it treated quickly. Whenever I treat patients with severe mental illnesses, I tend to estimate the length of time it will take them to get better by how long they have been ill. Someone who has only just started to suffer symptoms usually recovers in a few weeks, whereas those that have been ill for years can take months.

Alcoholic hallucinosis usually happens to someone who has been drinking excessively for some time and is continuing to drink. In a state of clear consciousness – that is, without any signs of drowsiness, incoordination or impaired memory – he starts to hear voices when nobody is there. He may hear other sounds or even see visions, but hearing voices is the most common symptom. Typically, these take the form of one or more people saying hostile and derogatory things to the sufferer, such as 'You are evil' or 'You are going to die'. Sometimes the voices are more friendly than this and the sufferer comes to accept them as friends. Usually, though, the victim is alarmed at this development, as one would expect, and recognizes that he is ill.

If treatment is not sought at this point and the condition progresses, this insight is gradually lost. Eventually, he comes to believe that the voices are real and may even believe what they say. Naturally, he then becomes paranoid, fearing all sorts of imaginary events that the voice(s) have described. He may become deluded, holding unshakeably a set of false beliefs and gradually elaborating on them in an increasingly bizarre way to make sense of his experiences.

One patient had a voice continually telling him he was guilty. In fact, he had been feeling guilty about the extent of his drinking and its effect on his family. He wondered what the voice was referring to and found his answer when he read of a particularly terrible murder in the local newspaper. He came to medical attention after he had confessed to the crime. Luckily, it didn't take the police long to recognize that he was ill rather than guilty. The timing was fortunate because he was on the verge of committing suicide.

There is a happy ending to this story. It took a while to get him better, using an alcohol-withdrawal regime, antipsychotic medication and a lot of counselling, but he is now completely well and a leading light in AA. He is well aware, though, that if he ever drinks to excess again, he is at risk of falling into this nightmare once more.

Stroke

A stroke occurs when blood supply is lost to a part of the brain either from haemorrhage (burst blood vessel) or from blockage of one of the blood vessels to the brain. The result is a loss of feeling and movement in whichever part of the body is controlled by that part of the brain or, if the stroke is in a part of the brain not concerned with feeling or movement, a range of other disabilities – for example, a loss of ability to speak clearly or to perform complex tasks.

Strokes occur much more commonly in very heavy drinkers than in the rest of the population. Recovery of lost function can often occur in time after a stroke, but it is clearly better to avoid this increased risk in the first place.

Pathological jealousy

Some experts nowadays doubt whether this syndrome is associated with alcoholism, but I have seen enough cases to be in no doubt. Certainly, it can occur in many other conditions, such as schizophrenia, but occasionally it crops up where the only disorder apparent in the patient's history is excessive drinking.

Pathological jealousy is the most dangerous condition known to psychiatrists. Violence and even murder are the not uncommon outcome. My advice to anyone living with a person who has this dreadful condition is unequivocal: temporarily remove yourself and alert the psychiatric services. When in doubt, seek advice from a doctor. Once the condition is treated, things will be safe again.

The first signs are increased suspiciousness by the sufferer of his partner/spouse. He starts to demand explanations of her whereabouts. He checks up on her and eventually starts to accuse her of infidelity. Soon he starts to produce spurious evidence, such as stains on her underclothes that he takes to be semen. A hair on the settee is brandished as belonging to her lover. His anger mounts and he may become violent in his demands for the truth. (The sex roles described here can just as easily be reversed.)

Of course, jealousy arises in all sorts of settings and doesn't of itself signify illness. A degree of jealousy, often without foundation, is often found in normal marriages. The essential element in abnormal jealousy is that it is of such a degree that all reason is lost, the person is convinced and completely consumed with their irrational belief and 'proofs', and acts on their conviction without reason. The situation is very dangerous and urgent treatment is essential.

As you can imagine, this condition is difficult to diagnose and easy to simulate on the part of the partner of the 'patient'. Caution before jumping to conclusions and sympathetic understanding are needed from anyone involved.

Cerebellar damage

The cerebellum is a wonderful organ (see Figure 7.3); it never ceases to amaze me. It is only small and is dwarfed by the brain, which sits directly above it, but it is every bit as marvellous as its clever neighbour in terms of its computing power.

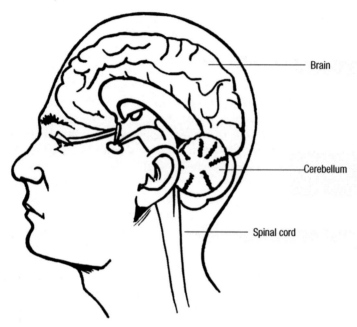

Figure 7.3 The brain and cerebellum

The cerebellum controls the measurement of movements and hence fine co-ordination. The best example that I have ever seen of its action was when, some years ago, I was unfortunate enough to be on a cross-Channel ferry in a force nine storm. In order to take my mind off my nausea, which was at risk of causing me embarrassment, I concentrated on a man on the other side of the cabin. He was playing darts, very successfully. Well, better than I can do it on dry land, anyway, though that may not be saying much.

As I watched this performance I wondered at the sophistication of a system that could, while being moved unpredictably in three dimensions, project an object using an arm that is restricted to two-dimensional movement, across a void of 8 feet into a space (the treble 20) about the size of a paper-clip.

This stunning feat deserved recognition, but I resisted the temptation to congratulate the athlete on the excellence of his cerebellum as I feared he might take this compliment the wrong way. Incidentally, it used to be assumed that darts could only be played well with 'a few bevvies' on board. This has now been disproved. The British Darts Association some years ago banned alcohol from use by all professional players during tournaments. Since this rule came into effect, average scores have not fallen and may even be increasing.

Though most of us don't have a cerebellum of quite this standing, it is none the less essential to our day-to-day functioning. Have you ever considered, for example, the complexity required to take a single step? You start by shifting your weight forwards. You then bend your right knee and raise it from the hip while shifting your weight slightly (but not too much) to the left. Then you push off by straightening your left foot and bracing the toes, while shifting the weight back slightly to the right. As your weight falls forward, you avoid falling flat on your face by straightening your right knee so that the right foot hitting the ground halts forward rotation of your body. Finally, at the moment that your centre of gravity moves forward of centre, you again shift your weight to the right and bend the left hip ready to take the next step. If you try to perform this movement consciously you could do yourself a serious injury. Fortunately, it is all done for you expertly by your cerebellum.

Excessive alcohol consumption can damage your cerebellum. If you add to this the fact that the victim will often suffer from peripheral nerve damage (see Chapter 7), rendering hands and feet numb, you will appreciate how disabling this condition can be. You may have seen a chap lurching along the pavement, walking with an exaggerated, rolling gait and stamping his feet down at each step. His bizarre and uncoordinated movements make him appear drunk, though he is in fact sober. He may be suffering from cerebellar damage. His incurable disability not only makes it impossible for him to live independently, but also causes him to be shunned by society, which is frightened by his apparent intoxication. He is often institutionalized.

Well, you will be glad to hear that that is the end of the tale of woe. I'll now go on to some more positive things, but before I do let me stress again that none of this will happen to you if you drink sensibly.

Part 4

SOME HELP WITH CUTTING DOWN OR DOING WITHOUT BOOZE

A lot of what I have said in this book is about the importance of drinking sensibly, or if you have had a drink problem, then cutting it out altogether. In Part 2, I pointed out that the key to overcoming a drink problem is to understand why you developed it. What follows is some general advice that may be of help to people with drink problems, but I hope will also be helpful for everyone else. Learning and practising these measures should make life more enjoyable and lower the risk of turning to alcohol as a way of dealing with problems and stress.

8

Sleep and relaxation

Sleep tips

I have lost count of how many of my patients cite poor sleep as the main reason for their drinking. Of course, for many of these people their excessive drinking predated their insomnia; they have mistaken the long-term sleep-wrecking effects of alcohol for an innate inability to sleep. However, some people genuinely don't sleep well and turn to alcohol in a vain effort to gain rest. These tips are aimed at this latter group.

Sleep needs

Many people assume that they need eight hours' sleep a night. Though some people do, many don't.

Sleep needs – as with most other individual characteristics – vary throughout the population (see Figure 8.1).

Though many people require between six and nine hours' sleep a night, some require ten or more, and others need five or less. Those

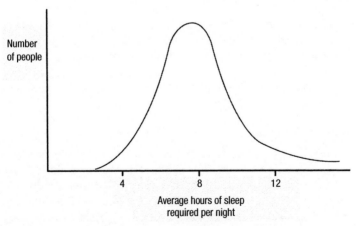

Figure 8.1 The normal distribution of sleep requirement in a population

whose bodies are programmed to sleep fewer than eight hours a night may assume that they sleep badly. In fact, they sleep well and can function perfectly adequately with this small amount.

The trick is to accept this and use the extra time available to your advantage. It was said that Margaret Thatcher needed only about four hours' sleep a night during her time as Prime Minister and, though you may not like what she did, you have to admit that she did a lot of it. She did much of her paperwork at night, which allowed her to adopt her particularly hands-on approach to leadership during the day. I would advocate this practical use of available time to anyone who has a low sleep need.

You need less sleep as you get older (see Figure 8.2).

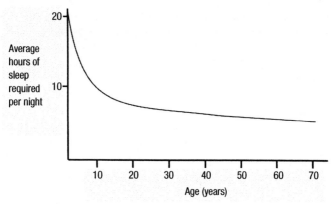

Figure 8.2 Average sleep requirement versus age

In your first year of life you will probably (and hopefully for your parents' sake) spend over sixteen hours a day asleep. At the age of twenty, the average is still over eight hours, but by the age of seventy this has fallen to around five hours. If an older person tries to sleep for as long as he did in his teens, he will be very frustrated and assume that he is suffering from poor sleep.

Catnaps and siestas

Your total sleep requirement is the total over a 24–hour period. If you sleep for a couple of hours during the day, the total sleep you can expect the next night will fall by two hours. The loss usually occurs in the first half of the night, so it feels as if you can't get to sleep at the time that you feel you should. In fact, your usual 11 p.m. has just been delayed to around 1 a.m. If you get upset about this, sleep may be delayed further (see below).

If you regularly sleep off a lunchtime drinking session, your sleep at night will be even more disturbed because of the rebound increase in anxiety and tension as the alcohol goes out of your system. Dealing with this by drinking in the evening as well will lead you into a vicious circle of increasingly wrecked sleep.

The effect of short-term sleep loss

You have got an important meeting tomorrow at which you have to give a difficult presentation. 'I must get a good night's sleep so that I am at my best. I know that so-and-so from head office is going to give me a hard time, so I'll have to be on my toes,' you say to yourself. Instead of your usual midnight bedtime you retire at 9.30 p.m.

The trouble is that you have a biological clock inside you that is set for sleep at around midnight. You lie in bed and concentrate hard on getting to sleep. After ten minutes you are still awake. You redouble your efforts. Your eyes are clamped shut, your jaw juts out, your neck veins protrude, and your face contorts into a picture of tense concentration with your efforts to sleep. This is a suitable attitude for a fight to the death with a grizzly bear, but not for slumber.

The clock shows 11 p.m. 'Oh no! I'm hardly going to get any more sleep than usual, I *must* get to sleep.' You are tense and aroused. As midnight passes you begin to get really worried. 'I'm going to be a wreck tomorrow, it will be a disaster.' You toss and turn until the early hours, when eventually fatigue overcomes your state of arousal and you sink into a troubled sleep. You sleep through the alarm and arrive late for the meeting, flustered and weary. Your worst fears have come true and the man from head office has a ball at your expense.

If only you had realized this simple fact: one night's sleep loss does not affect your performance one iota. It wasn't the lost sleep that spoilt your presentation; it was the fact that you spent the night worrying about not sleeping. Worry and tension are very wearing. Adrenaline

has been pumping around your body all night, so that at the time you needed it, for the meeting, there was none left and you were exhausted.

There have been lots of studies that have confirmed this. Subjects are deprived of a night's sleep and then tested on a range of mental and manual skills. They perform just as well as subjects who have been given a full night's sleep, but because the test results are of no concern to them they haven't worried about their sleep loss.

Of course, if you are deprived of sleep regularly, you do suffer. I remember when I was a houseman (a first-year junior doctor – the dogsbody) once having a particularly busy weekend on call and in those days the hours were pretty extreme. I didn't get to bed from Friday morning to Monday evening. I was OK for the first part of the weekend, but Sunday night was tough and I am told that on Monday afternoon I arrived for the ward round looking perplexed and asked where I was and why I was here. Fortunately, with the new rules on doctors' hours, this rarely occurs nowadays, but it was an interesting if alarming experience of the effects of repeated sleep deprivation.

Presuming that you are not unfortunate enough to have this kind of job, my best advice is to have a regular time to go to bed and to stick to it. If you can't sleep on one particular night, don't worry. Instead, practise a relaxation exercise (see below). Effective relaxation confers many of the restorative benefits of sleep and will allow you to be fighting fit the next day, whether you sleep well or not.

Tea and coffee

Most Britons drink a lot of coffee and/or tea. Both contain caffeine, a stimulant drug with similar, though much weaker, effects to amphetamine. Another memory of mine is of burning the midnight oil when revising for my final medical exams. I had a filter coffee machine: the type that sits in a glass jug on a hotplate to keep the coffee warm. As I worked through the night, I drank my way through several jugs of this brew. What I hadn't realized was that, when left to stand, the water was being lost from the coffee in the jug through heating, so the stuff that I was drinking was super-strength. At about 2 a.m. I started to feel strange. The symptoms were of anxiety, restlessness, slight tremor, palpitations and an inability to think straight. When I went to bed I was unable to sleep. I was suffering from caffeine intoxication, and most unpleasant it was too.

It is often the custom to finish an evening meal with strong coffee. Many people have several cups in an evening. This is enough to spoil your sleep as caffeine hangs around in your body for several hours. If you have difficulty sleeping, it is wise to have your last cup before 5 p.m. Also look out for some soft drinks. Many contain caffeine in considerable amounts.

As an aside, I believe that many people are addicted to coffee. Try sometime going a whole working day without a cup. You may well feel tired, lethargic and unable to think with your usual clarity. This is caffeine withdrawal. People who have abandoned coffee and tea or turned to decaffeinated brands often say that they feel a lot better for it.

A hot milky drink

The manufacturers of Horlicks and other malted beverages have long extolled their virtues in assisting good sleep. Most of us treat this claim sceptically, but in fact it is based on sound scientific facts. The benefits of these drinks can mostly be gained by a cup of hot milk, but, for most people, malted drinks taste better.

Milk is rich in protein, carbohydrate and fat. The presence of these foods in the gut draws blood supply there. Also, you will have noticed how blood supply is increased to a part of the body that is warmed. If you put your hand in hot water it goes pink. Drinking hot milk does the same for the gut.

Though the brain's blood supply is pretty well protected, the increased blood supply passing to the stomach and intestines causes a slight fall in the supply to the brain. This is part of what causes the drowsiness that helps you go to sleep after your bedtime milky drink. Unlike the sleep-inducing effects of alcohol, this effect keeps going undiminished year after year. Try it and see.

Exercise

The body uses sleep as a way of recuperating after the physical (and mental) rigours of the day. If there haven't been any rigours, sleep is deemed unnecessary. To sleep soundly, it is wise to take some exercise every day. Jumping in and out of the car and raising the glass to your lips do not count. Regular exercise (taken sensibly, according to your level of fitness) is, of course, good for your health anyway, and there is increasing evidence that it helps combat stress and improve your mood. In particular, aerobic exercise taken out of doors seems to help with circadian rhythms and is protective against seasonal affective disorder (SAD).

Heat and ventilation

It may seem to be wasteful to have the heating on and the bedroom window open, but this can be very helpful for sleep. Being very hot or cold inhibits sleep, as does a stuffy atmosphere. It is surprising how high the carbon dioxide concentration can get in a room with windows and door closed and two people sleeping in it. This stale air tends to retard falling asleep and cause interruptions in the pattern of sleep through the night.

Meals

Eating at regular times helps to develop a pattern that the body clock can follow. Of course, this isn't always possible if you have a job with irregular hours or are looking after a baby, but the nearer you can get to a regular pattern of eating times, the better your sleep is likely to be. The same applies to other aspects of your life. An uncertain life-style without any routine does not encourage the body to develop the rhythms that lead to a regular sleep–wake cycle. It is important, as far as possible, to go to bed at roughly the same time most evenings and to retire neither hungry nor over-full.

Books, television, etc.

It is unfortunate that the television companies tend to put on horror films and cops-and-robbers shows late at night, presumably because this stuff is an ideal filler for a time when most people have gone

to bed. Watching such programmes can seriously damage your sleep because, whatever its quality, it is arousing, with lots of death and destruction and the obligatory ploys to make you jump out of your seat just when you thought the hero/heroine was safe. Another annoying thing that I have noticed is that late-night television announcers (and weather forecasters) talk to you as if you were a two-year-old child. This high-pitched smiling patter makes my blood boil! If it does the same to you, I would suggest turning the sound down in between programmes.

The brain is not designed to pass rapidly from a state of high arousal to sleep, so anything exciting, annoying or upsetting is likely to delay the onset of sleep. The same is true of books. I would advise against thrillers at bedtime for this reason. Go for something less exciting – a magazine, perhaps. For the last twenty years I have been reading *A la recherche du temps perdu* ('remembrance of times past') by Marcel Proust (in English – I'm terrible at languages) at the rate of half a page every now and again. It is a lovely book, beautifully written, with touches of soft humour, but nothing whatever has happened in it yet. I'm on page 460 and, at around 6,000 pages, I think that it should last longer than me.

A warning here about bringing work home with you. One insomniac assured me that he had supper at 8.30 every evening and then curled up for a couple of hours to read before going to bed at 11 p.m., but still he couldn't sleep. On closer questioning, it emerged that what he was reading was journals on investment and the daily markets in order to maximize his profits as a stockbroker and to steal a march on his fellow brokers in the morning. He admitted to 'getting a real buzz out of it'. Anyone who has studied knows that it takes a great deal of concentration and effort. You need at least a couple of hours' relaxing or doing something useless before your brain will be ready to sleep.

Sex

This is sometimes a major source of discord between couples. After sex, most women become more alert, while most men tend to fall asleep. This isn't true for all men and women, but it is for many. The contrast is due to different effects of sexual intercourse on the nervous system of the two sexes and has become the source of many a gag for comedians, professional and amateur. For insomniac men (and occasionally women), this fact can be a useful point to take into account when considering the evening's agenda. Approach this carefully, though; an invitation such as 'How about it, then, because I want a good night's sleep' just won't do.

No planning at bedtime

You've had a very busy day; no time to think. I know it well. You get home late, have supper, have a chat and go to bed. At last you have the time and space to review the day and think of what is needed for tomorrow. Suddenly you remember some essential task and you are worried that you will forget it by the morning. You work the problem through in your mind and it worries you because this problem throws up a whole load of others. Now you have *several* problems instead of one and you try to sort them out and log them in your brain so that you will remember what you have to do tomorrow. Then you try to go to sleep, but you can't.

It's hardly surprising. How can you expect to sleep when you have programmed your brain to solve problems? The trouble is that if you try to exclude these thoughts from your mind they keep popping back. However hard you try, you can't clear your mind ready for slumber.

The brain is like that. It won't let something rest until it is sorted out or at least put somewhere. It's like a pop-up on your computer. So file the pop-up in a different place.

Keep a notepad by your bed. Every time a thought or problem comes into your head, write it down. Also write down a time in the morning when you will work out your plan to sort out each problem. For example, 7.30–8.00 a.m. sort out problems – 1) agenda for meeting 2) sort out holiday arrangements 3) phone bank manager about overdraft.

By putting your thoughts on to paper, you take them out of your brain; but your brain will continue to 'worry' unless you reassure it

with a guarantee of a time when all will be made right. Of course, when you look at your problem list in the morning it may look less urgent and not worth considering. None the less, consider the list you must, because otherwise your brain won't believe you the next time you write such a list and will go back to producing pop-ups again.

Forgiveness

As I have said, many people use bedtime as a time to reflect on the day. You tend to focus on the annoying parts. You remember the incidents when someone was rude or somehow got one over on you. 'If only I had been quicker,' you muse, 'I could have given a clever reply. That would have really put him in his place.' So you plan out what pithy aphorism you are going to throw at him tomorrow. All of this gets you quite worked up and, of course, you can't sleep.

This is a complete waste of time because rarely in the history of human experience has anyone been known to carry through the plan the next day. When the morning comes, it all seems trivial, and to seek the person out just to vent your spleen would be very silly. The fact is that in the darkness and solitude of the night issues and feelings become magnified and only the next day do they resume realistic proportions.

So, in order to sleep well the rule is that everyone is forgiven everything at night-time. This takes some practice but can be done. The next day, you can lay plans for murder if you wish; that is entirely your affair. But no recriminations at night.

Paradoxical injunction

This is based on the established psychological principle that many people unconsciously tend to resist instructions or orders, whoever they come from. They are not trying to be awkward, the mind just works that way. Sometimes a therapist will help someone to change an entrenched behaviour by giving them the opposite instruction from what is really desired, in order to overcome this resistance.

I have experienced this myself. When studying for exams, I always found that the prospect of getting down to a solid session of work made me feel like going to sleep. The more urgently I told myself that I must do it, the sleepier I felt. This was strange because it could happen even in the middle of the morning. As soon as the exam was over I would never feel sleepy in the morning; to try to sleep then would be impossible. My brain was unconsciously resisting my order to work.

This phenomenon can be used to your advantage. Choose your least favourite task (for me it would be ironing) and timetable it for about an hour after your usual bedtime. The prospect of the task may cause you to be asleep by the appointed time. If not, then time when you would otherwise have been uselessly fretting in bed will be put to good use. The achievement of this chore will tend to make you more relaxed and help you to sleep afterwards.

For the majority of people, using these tips significantly improves their sleep. If you are still sleeping badly, consult your doctor. Though occasionally they are needed (take your doctor's advice on this), on the whole it is worth avoiding sleeping pills. Though they increase sleep in the short term, in the long run, if taken regularly, they make the problem worse; and, as most of them are potentially addictive, they may add this to your difficulties. If you have to use sleeping pills, don't use them every night unless instructed to do so. Going at least two nights a week without any pills will greatly reduce the risk of addiction.

Finally, whatever you do, never use alcohol as an aid to sleep. This is how a lot of people develop their drink problem, and once you have come to rely on a drink to sleep, you are trapped, needing ever more to sleep and becoming ever more addicted as a result.

Relaxation

The other most common cause for people turning to drink is that they are tense and anxious. Alcohol gives short-term relief but, as explained earlier, it compounds the problem in the long run.

The best way to combat stress is to learn and become expert at a relaxation exercise. There are many variations on this theme and the thing is to find the one that works best for you. There are several relaxation CDs and programs commercially available and many people find it easiest to learn the techniques by listening to one of these. Others get benefit from yoga techniques learnt in a group setting. Some find that following a written set of instructions helps them better, by allowing them to do the exercise at their own pace with their own mental imagery. What follows is just one example of such a technique, but one that many of my patients have found helpful.

Whichever exercise you choose, the essential point is that it needs a lot of practice. Though a few people pick it up very quickly, for the majority, relaxation exercises are a complete waste of time to begin with. Some people even feel worse at the beginning, because doing anything and having it fail tends to make you feel tense.

However, persevere because when you really master the technique you will find that it changes your life, allowing you to deal with situations that previously you could not have coped with at all. The people who get benefit from relaxation exercises are those who put them top of their list of priorities and practise for at least half an hour every day, come hell or high water.

Looking back, I did relaxation exercises every day for about two and a half years. I had to because I had a panic attack in my first ever Viva exam at medical school. These old chaps were peering over their half-rim specs, firing questions at me and I simply froze. Fortunately, the university allowed me to redo the exam a year later, by which point I had got good enough at the exercise effectively to pre-treat myself and I got through OK. It took me about a month of daily practice for the exercise to be any use at all. It took at least six months to get to the stage of being able to use it when under pressure, because the most difficult time to do a relaxation exercise effectively is when you most need it, at times of high stress. In about two to three years I got to the stage of no longer needing the exercise because I could switch on the relaxed state like a light when necessary. The average is about nine months to get to this stage, so I'm a bit slow, but who cares? I can tell you that gaining this ability is worth all the time and effort. There is no limit to how good you can get at this if you keep practising. You may have seen the clip of a Buddhist monk who puts a knitting needle through both of his cheeks, extracts it, and then demonstrates to the camera that the holes do not bleed. He is so good at controlling his bodily functions that he can move his blood around his body at will. I don't suggest that you try this at home, but you can get good enough to deal with your anxiety without resorting to alcohol.

A relaxation exercise

Spend 15–30 minutes on this exercise.

1 Find a suitable place to relax. A bed or an easy chair is ideal, but anywhere will do, preferably quiet and private. If your chair in the office or a house full of children is all there is, it can still be done.
2 As far as you can, try to clear your mind of thoughts.
3 Take three very slow, very deep breaths (10–15 seconds to breathe in and out once).
4 Imagine a neutral figure. An example might be the number 1. Don't choose any object or figure with an emotional significance, such as a ring or a person, for example. Let it fill your mind. See it in your mind's eye, give it a colour, try to see it in 3-D and repeat it to yourself, under your breath, many times over. Continue until it fills your mind.

5 Slowly change to imagine yourself in a quiet, peaceful and pleasurable place or situation. This may be a favourite place or situation, or a pleasant scene from your past. Be there, and notice all the feelings, in each sense. See it, feel it, hear it, taste it and smell it. Spend some time there.*

6 Slowly change to be aware of your body. Notice any tension. Take each group of muscles in turn, and tense them, then relax them two or three times each. Include fingers, hands, arms, shoulders, neck, face, chest, tummy, buttocks, thighs, legs, feet and toes. Be aware of the feeling of relaxation. When complete, spend some time in this relaxed state.

7 Slowly get up and go about your business.

Don't hurry this procedure and remember to practise. It will work.

---

* For example, if you are imagining that you are on a beach, what direction is the wind blowing from? What does your suntan lotion smell of? Are you sweating? Does the temperature change when a cloud covers the sun? Is the sand hard or soft? What are you eating and what does it taste of? Are the palm trees the stumpy-type ones or tall coconut palms? If the latter, are the coconuts green or brown? This isn't just an image, it's a multisensory experience.

9

Other useful techniques

Thought-stopping

When you are stressed you often find that a thought sticks in your mind and you can't get rid of it. If you try to clear it out of your mind it keeps coming back, and mulling it over time and again makes you even more tense. The following technique, again with practice, can help you to clear your mind so that you can get on with what you are doing or think about something else. This ability is an important part of stress management, which is an essential skill in beating addiction to alcohol.

When you are alone, suddenly make a loud noise. Remember the sudden sensation.

When you find yourself mulling over repetitive thoughts, bring this memory into your mind. Allow it to give you a jolt.

Say sharply to yourself: '*Stop*'. This does not have to be out loud, but imagine yourself saying it sharply and loudly.

Substitute another thought that is relevant and realistic in your situation, or go and do something that requires concentration.

Problem-solving

The trouble with problems is that they don't come one at a time but, like buses, in batches. When you are in one of these spells, the weight of problems seems so overwhelming that you don't know where to

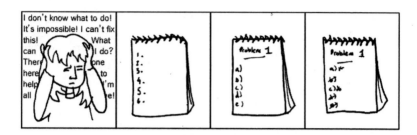

start. The whole thing seems like a gigantic mess and you might be forgiven for feeling like having a drink and forgetting about it for a while. Of course, through inaction the problems just seem to get bigger.

The principle of problem-solving is simple: take a set of problems or one big problem and split it up into smaller pieces. Let's take an example. You are in a financial mess. This problem is too big to manage as a whole, so split it up:

1 I'm above my overdraft limit at the bank.
2 My creditors are getting insistent.
3 I'm spending beyond my means.
4 My debtors aren't paying up.
5 The mortgage rate has gone up.
6 The car is on its last legs.
7 Christmas is just around the corner.

Now you have a set of smaller and more manageable problems to sort out. Take each one in turn and 'brainstorm' some possible actions. This means including all your ideas on what to do – the apparently bad ones as well as the obviously sensible ones. For example, for problem 1 a possible list might be:

a Ask the manager to extend my overdraft limit.
b Tell him/her that the problem is largely one of cash flow, that I am addressing it, and it should only be temporary.
c Take out a short-term loan.
d Borrow from friends/relatives.
e Cut out items of expenditure (see problem 3).
f Ignore it.
g Do more overtime.
h Move house.
i Change job.

Now think each option through and reject those that don't work. Talk it through with someone, if this helps.

Do this process for each of the points that you originally listed. Several of the action points will recur. Gather them together and then put them in a list of priority and act on them one at a time. Tick them off as you do each one. The process of working through the list is very satisfying and allows you to feel that you are doing everything that can be done to improve the situation.

Of course, following this structure for problems does not make them go away, but it does give you more control over them. Stress, and drinking to cope with it, tends to happen when you feel that you have lost all control over your life.

Time management

I tend to rush around at a hundred miles an hour, not always achieving a lot. When it was suggested to me that I was stressing myself unnecessarily and that I needed a time-management program, I protested: 'It isn't that I don't manage my time, there just isn't enough time to do everything.' However, a kindly person ignored my protestations and designed a time plan for me anyway. This involved organizing my day so that I was doing tasks together that could be done in one place, pulling together blocks of time for paperwork, and having slots through the week left empty for emergencies and

	Monday	Tuesday	Wednesday	Thursday	Friday	Saturday	Sunday
9 am		spare for crisis and problems		filing	deliver report	shopping	↑
10 am	admin meeting	personal work	computer work	travel
11 am			
12 am		prepare reports	meet with client
1 pm		L	U N	C H			rest
2 pm	personal work	travelling	presentation	meeting about report	travel personal work	rest	
3 pm	meeting	rest
4 pm		travelling	admin	prepare next week's time plan
5 pm				↓
Evening	rest	prepare presentation	late meeting	going out	rest	theatre	

Figure 9.1 A time plan

unforeseen circumstances. As a result, I am getting through a lot more work and am much less stressed. The only bit of it I don't like is being proved wrong.

If you find yourself harassed and overburdened, I would strongly recommend that you draw up a weekly time plan, with spaces for unforeseen events and for rest (see Figure 9.1). This works even for the most irregular of lifestyles, such as bringing up children.

Acting as if

As mentioned earlier in the book, many people are aware of aspects of themselves that they would like to change, but assume that this is impossible. 'You can't change your personality' or 'You can't teach an old dog new tricks' are frequently heard justifications for this way of thinking.

The fact is that you can change, simply by acting as if you were the way you would like to be. This isn't easy, but it can be done with persistence. For instance, if you want to be more outgoing, emulate someone who is. You will not do it very well at first and may feel rather gauche, but in time you will become the genuine article, being and feeling outgoing.

For example, I used to be addicted to sport on TV. I couldn't imagine getting through an English winter without the rugby internationals on TV to look forward to. However, as my lifestyle and responsibilities changed, it became impossible to devote so much time to watching sport. At first I missed it terribly and resented whatever I was doing while the international was on the box, but over time I got used to it and now, by choice, I will only watch the rugby if there isn't anything better to do. My interests and values have changed in line with my behaviour.

If you want to be someone who doesn't drink and doesn't want to drink, look at the lifestyles of other non-drinkers. Mostly you will see that they enjoy life every bit as much as drinking friends. Try emulating aspects of their lifestyle that you would like to develop yourself. You are a lot more adaptable and changeable than you think.

Thinking styles

There is a whole area of psychotherapy (Cognitive Behavioural Therapy – CBT) based on the observation that people who learn to think in a self-defeating and depressive way tend to become depressed. Sometimes they drink. I can only touch on this enormous subject here, but I will mention some of the thinking patterns that I often see in my patients.

Many people have deep inside the feeling that 'I am no good', 'I will always fail', 'nobody will like me' or 'sooner or later I will be found out'. The last of these self-statements is particularly interesting to me. In the face of success, frequent praise, loving friends and considerable competence, people often still feel that what they do or who they are is somehow not worthwhile or not as good as other people. Adults often feel that they are really still children in an adults' world, that other people are the real grown-ups, while they are just pretending. Anything they achieve is automatically discounted. I call this 'The Marx Effect' after Groucho Marx who produced the lovely line: 'I wouldn't want to be a member of a club that would have me as a member'. What these folks don't realize is that the other people that they look up to probably feel the same way themselves.

People who are happy and fulfilled tend to look at the world and themselves objectively. If you don't, and particularly if you tend to think in the way I have described, it is worth paying some attention to your thinking.

Whenever you feel low, stop and consider what is going through your mind. If it involves pessimistic thoughts or running yourself down, stop yourself for a moment. What is a more objective way of looking at the situation? How would a more confident or optimistic friend evaluate it? If your pessimistic way of looking at it does not hold up to scrutiny, then abandon it and search for what is the realistic interpretation.

Let's take an example. Your boss has not looked at you when you passed him (yes, I know your boss could just as easily be a woman) in the corridor and he failed to acknowledge your greeting. You may assume that he is displeased with you. The depressive thinking pattern would continue from here. 'He's probably found something that I have done wrong, I'll probably get sacked, I knew this would happen, I'd be found out eventually, because I'm no good and I always fail.' Written down, this train of thought looks ridiculous, but many people habitually think this way.

Of course, the boss was actually just preoccupied and didn't notice you. When nothing nasty happens in ensuing days and in fact a pay rise arrives, the depressive thinker does not recognize that his fears were groundless and determine to be more realistic next time, he just forgets it. But if he is actually criticized, as all of us are from time to time, he says to himself, 'There we are, then. I knew it, this proves I am useless.'

It really is worth checking occasionally that you are thinking realistically. Incidentally, I don't go for 'positive thinking'. This seems to me to be primarily an invention to persuade inadequate sportspeople to go out and get beaten up by bigger opposition under the misapprehension that 'we are the best'. This sort of unrealistic optimism is soon shown up and tends to lead to disillusionment (or injury). But thinking realistically is essential to a happy lifestyle.

There are other thinking errors often found in people with drink problems. Denial is the most common, and I have dealt with it in an earlier chapter. In the face of everyone around saying or implying that he is drinking too much, the drinker holds that he 'just has a tipple'. It is important to listen to what your friends and family are saying and to act on it. One phrase that makes my heart sink when I hear it from someone with a drink problem is 'I'll do it my way'. This isn't to say that I am always right in what I advise but, in my experience, someone whose drink problem has gone so far as to need treatment, and who nevertheless ignores advice on how to conquer it, usually ends up drinking even more.

Projection refers to the tendency to spend a lot of time looking into the future, creating imaginary scenarios that will probably never happen. Not only does this add unnecessarily to your problems, but it prevents you from really living now. Another is 'I mustn't let myself feel bad/depressed/pain, etc.' It is a short step from this to 'I need a drink to get me through'. In fact, it is realistic to say 'I'm feeling bad this evening, but if I put up with it and don't drink, I will feel better in the morning.' Finally, the statement 'I mustn't do anything that I might fail at' is the most handicapping of all. Allowing yourself to try and fail without self-recrimination is very liberating and opens up a world of experience and opportunity. Every happy and successful person I have ever met is able to fail without beating himself up. Look, for example, at successful sportspeople – in particular from one of my sports, cricket. The greatest batsmen sometimes get out to bad shots, but you can see as they walk off that they don't take this as a catastrophe. They just learn from their mistake for next time, while lesser players are scared of failing because they dread the self-recrimination that will follow if they do. So inevitably they do fail. Treat yourself kindly when you fail, but learn from your mistakes.

Drug treatments

Antabuse: This is a medication that is sometimes useful in people recovering from alcoholism. If taken once a day, it removes the temptation to drink, because it sets up a very unpleasant chemical reaction to alcohol. If you have a drink while on antabuse, you will feel ill and nauseous, get a headache, and develop red blotches on your skin. Knowing this is a strong disincentive to drink. Of course, it only works if you want to stop drinking, as all you have to do to have a drink is to stop taking the drug for a few days. However, some people find only having to make the decision to abstain from alcohol once a day, at the time you take the tablet, is much easier than constantly holding on against the urge to drink through the day.

Some cautions. Antabuse cannot be used if your liver function is impaired (a few experts disagree with this), so you may need to cope for a while without it during the period that your liver is recovering.

Everyone's sensitivity to antabuse is different. While everyone should beware of taking alcohol in any form while on antabuse – for example, in medicines, mouthwash, food or liqueur chocolates – a few people will get a reaction even to the smell of alcohol, such as in a kitchen where alcohol is used in the cooking.

To my mind, antabuse is dangerous in very impulsive individuals. If you are someone who is liable to say, 'To hell with it, I am going to have a drink whatever the result' and then drink half a bottle of Scotch in five minutes while taking antabuse, the reaction could be very serious and even fatal. You would do better to avoid antabuse altogether.

Antabuse is only available on prescription. Seek the advice of your doctor.

Campral (Acamprosate): This drug is designed to take the edge off craving. It can be helpful for people who are tormented by frequent spells of severe craving, but who are motivated to maintain abstinence from alcohol. Obviously, it should not be used by those who are trying a controlled drinking approach and should be stopped if a relapse into drinking occurs. It is usually taken for around six months or so. Some find it very helpful, though in my experience most relapses don't occur through spells of craving, but rather follow failure to keep going the measures that led to success in the first place.

Nalorex (Naltrexone): This drug has been used for some years to help heroin addicts stay abstinent. It works by stopping opiate drugs such as heroin from having any effect, through blocking the sites at which these drugs act. It is now being used by some to help achieve abstinence from alcohol.

The rationale is that Naltrexone also blocks the action of the body's own opiates, the endorphins. These chemicals reduce pain and discomfort and increase pleasure and enjoyment.

The idea is that initially you continue drinking while taking the drug. Because the endorphins are blocked you get no pleasure from drinking. After a predetermined period (weeks), both the drug and drinking stops. Activities that used to give pleasure are then reintroduced. As the endorphin system is now active again, these non-addictive activities are rewarded by pleasure. In theory, through the principles of conditioning, this should encourage non-drinking behaviours and make it easier to abstain.

Big claims are being made for treatments, including the use of Naltrexone, though only time will tell whether it will prove useful.

The drink diary

It is a good idea for everyone to know how much they are drinking. Try keeping a diary of everything that you drink throughout a week (see Figure 9.2).

Put the amounts down in units, using the table of units printed earlier in this book. At the end of the week add up the units. If the total is above the safe limit, repeat the exercise each week, attempting to get down to a safe level. If necessary, keep the diary going to make sure that you are sticking to safe levels.

	Monday	Tuesday	Wednesday	Thursday	Friday	Saturday	Sunday
Lunchtime		2		2		4	4
Evening	3	2	3 before dinner 4 at dinner 3 after dinne		6	6	
Total units	3	6	10	2	6	10	4

Weekly total units = 41

Figure 9.2 A drink diary

Remember, though, that if you have ever had a drink problem serious enough to require treatment, there is no safe limit and it would be prudent to cut out the booze completely.

Cueing

Sadly, many people who really want to stop drinking relapse after treatment. A few of these seem to do so by accident. Of course, in anybody who returns to drinking, there is a part of him that wants to, but quite often it appears that this is an unconscious desire. Consciously he wants to remain abstinent, but the unconscious part of his mind takes him by surprise at an unexpected moment, and suddenly he has had a drink, then several, and before he knows it he has returned to the nightmare of dependence on alcohol.

The thing is to prevent the first drink by making sure that your conscious mind is always in control.

I suggest ensuring this by using the technique of cueing. What are the circumstances in which you used to drink and in which you would be at risk of a lapse? Did you buy your drink from the off-licence and drink it at home? If so, arriving at the door of an off-licence would then be a cue.

As you stop at the door of any off-licence, always imagine an alarm bell ringing. This is your danger time. It is no good just saying to yourself at this point, 'I mustn't buy a drink', because, as mentioned in the section on paradoxical injunction, you may well instinctively rebel against such an order, with a rationalization such as 'Just one

can of beer won't do me any harm'. Instead, when the alarm bell rings in response to the cue, ask yourself this question: 'Am I about to buy myself a drink?'

If the answer is no, and you are going in, for example, to buy a box of chocolates, you can go straight on in and no time is lost by the exercise. However, if the answer is yes, there is another question to ask yourself: 'Is it worth it?'

Now time five minutes on your watch and make yourself take every minute of this in considering your answer. Take a walk along the road while you ponder the pros and cons. Of course, the cons greatly out-weigh the pros; your conscious mind knows that. If you truly want to remain sober, the craving for a drink should have passed or be on the wane by the time the five minutes are up (most cravings last only minutes, though you may get several in a day). At this point you make your decision whether to go in and buy a drink or not. If you decide not to, substitute another thought or action, such as 'I'll go and buy a newspaper'. You may find it helpful to substitute a rewarding action here, such as going to buy the treat that you have been hankering for. After all, you are saving a lot of money by not drinking. You deserve some rewards, though most people find that the main reward is in real-izing that they have conquered their cravings.

If you do decide to drink, it is because in all consciousness you want to, having considered the consequences. But this procedure will stop you from lapsing by mistake.

Make sure to practise this cueing system, so that the alarm bell rings on cue every time you enter your risk situation. Everyone's risk situations are different. In AA they talk about the acronym 'HALT', standing for: Hungry, Angry, Lonely, Tired. These are certainly common cues, but you will need to choose your own cue or cues with care, so that the alarm bell rings whenever you are in a situation that may lead to you having a drink.

The abstinence violation effect

For anyone who has had a drink problem, taking a drink is very dangerous and should be avoided at all costs. But having an 'accidental' lapse does not need to lead to a full relapse. It usually does, because of the abstinence violation effect. The train of thought goes like this:

'Oh no, I've taken a drink. After three weeks without a drop, I've gone and blown it. It's all ruined now, I haven't managed it, I might just as well get drunk.'

The next day, having been drunk the day before, you come to the same conclusion – In other words, because you haven't been completely successful, you might as well continue drinking. So you are back in the cycle of dependence. This did not need to happen. There were several points at which disaster could have been avoided. Even after you had the first sip, you could have thrown the rest away. After the first whole drink you could have stopped there. The next day you could have resolved to return to abstinence.

Sure, the lapse was dangerous and it would have been better if it hadn't happened, but if three weeks later you had been able to report 'I have been six weeks with just one lapse; I have learnt from that and I think I know how to prevent a recurrence', you will have done pretty well. You can put this period down in your diary as a relative success.

This is not a reason for allowing yourself 'just one drink', but the fact is that some people do manage to pull themselves back from the brink. A lapse does not have to turn into a full relapse.

The 'niceness defence' and the 'barrister's jeopardy'

Though people with drink problems, like others, come in all types, many of my favourite people are among the alcoholics I have treated as so many of them are really nice people.

While there is nothing whatever wrong with being nice, it can be used as a defence that prolongs problem drinking. 'I couldn't criticize Simon for being drunk. He's so nice, I wouldn't want to hurt him.' So Simon gets further down the path to alcoholism without being challenged. This doesn't do him any favours; in fact, in the long run, the sympathetic consideration of his friends causes him much more suffering than if he had been confronted the first time his drinking gave rise for concern.

The other disadvantaged group is those who are very intelligent, with a way with words. Some time ago, on reviewing my practice, I realized that I had treated ten barristers for addictions. Not one had succeeded in gaining long-term recovery. This was beyond statistical probability as our unit claims around a 50 per cent success rate (don't look at success rates too closely; each unit treats different types of people and defines 'success' differently). At first this was puzzling, but on reflection the reason was clear. Barristers are so good with words that they can persuade you, me and themselves of almost anything, including 'It's OK to have a drink', while a more intellectually limited person will be immediately and effectively challenged if he comes up with tosh like this.

The best way to help someone with a drink problem is to be honest. AA call it 'tough love'. You won't get any thanks for it, at least at first; but by drawing attention to the problem, you are offering the problem drinker an opportunity to tackle the problem before it is too late. If you are clever and verbal, put your cleverness away whenever you are talking or thinking about drink. Listen to others, not your own elegant logic.

Overconfidence

I see a lot of people who think that they can either give up drinking or control their drinking easily, just through their strength of will. These characters smile at me indulgently as I give them my advice. You can see them thinking, 'Yes, yes, I've heard it all before; don't these shrinks go on so! I'll manage, I always do. There's nothing and no one has

beaten me before. A little drink problem is no different, I'll sort it out my way.'

Ah, 'my way'. I think I have heard those words more times than the song has been sung and they make my heart sink.

This confidence is based on the misconception that a lone fight against alcoholism is an equal struggle. I use a metaphor to illustrate this: a man is standing on a beach looking out to sea. A gigantic 60-foot-high tsunami is approaching. As it nears and is looming over him, the man looks the wave up and down slowly and declares, 'Yes, I can handle that, no problem.'

Well, I'm sorry, my friend, you can't handle it and you're going to be swept away to a watery grave. That wave is several orders of magnitude bigger than you are. Your only chance is to run as fast as you can for high ground.

In the case of alcoholism, this high ground may come in a variety of forms of help. The most easily accessible is AA. The crucial point here, though, is don't make the mistake of thinking you can do it yourself through being big, strong and clever.

Staying present

Worry is often the cause of someone self-medicating with alcohol. It comes from spending too much time in self-recrimination for things you've got wrong in the past, or in fearing what you'll get wrong or lose in the future. This is why AA say 'Keep it in the day'. Don't worry about tomorrow or next week/month/year unless there's something you can do about it. If there is, do it, then get straight back into today. After all, the present is the only time with which we have direct contact, and so have any real influence over. It's impossible to be anxious if you are truly present. If you are anxious, try to observe your anxiety rather than getting so caught up with it. You'll see that in due course even the worst panic passes without anything dreadful having happened.

There is an offshoot of Cognitive Behavioural Therapy (CBT) called 'Mindfulness' which uses this principle, among others. It's also at the core of Ekhart Tolle's bestselling book *The Power of Now*. I highly recommend it, though you may want to gloss over some of the slightly 'New Agey' passages in it if that isn't your thing.

Talking

There are several opposites to alcoholism, two of which are *feeling* and *talking*. You drink alcohol to make your feelings go away, then it gets out of control and your feelings get worse. You avoid talking about the problem so as not to be challenged.

So if you feel bad, *feel bad*. Don't try to chase it away. It will pass. But do talk to someone about how you're feeling. Alcoholism is a disease that needs secrecy to flourish. Sharing your feelings with someone sober who you can trust is one of the strongest antidotes to the disease. Do this sharing when sober. The emotional outpourings of a drunk person are worth diddly-squat and won't be remembered anyway. Don't engage with anyone who is intoxicated. It's a waste of time.

If all of this seems like the ten commandments, I am sorry, but if any of it applies to you, you may find it useful to address it, if necessary with the help of a counsellor (ask your GP or look for a pamphlet in your GP's surgery – counselling services are available in most areas). If your needs are complex and particularly if you are physically addicted to alcohol, you may be referred to a psychiatrist. There are psychiatrists specializing in the treatment of alcoholism in almost every area and many have multidisciplinary teams of expert professionals who can arrange help pretty quickly. The way to access these services is first to see your GP.

10

The disease concept, AA and one member's experience

Worthy organization though they are, I am not referring here to the Automobile Association, but to Alcoholics Anonymous. This organization has helped more people with drink problems to turn their lives around than every other organization and service put together. If you feel you may have a problem, you could do a lot worse than to contact your local group first. Their contact number will be in your local telephone directory, or Google them. There is also a 24-hour national helpline – 0207 833 0022. AA is available 365 days a year. Many people have heard that it is religious and are put off going because of this. In my view this is not a valid reason for avoiding something that has helped so many people who would not regard themselves as 'religious'. They do indeed introduce the concept of a higher power that you need to turn to for strength, but I would suggest that even the most atheist among us recognizes that if a concept works in practice, it is worth running with it. AA works. The concept of God also appears in several of the steps, but what is mentioned is 'God, *as we understood him*', which allows a great deal of scope for personal interpretation. Some in AA who don't go for things spiritual refer to GOD as an acronym for 'Group of Drunks'. The point is that you won't succeed if you rely solely on your own wit and determination, but with the help of others who have been there, seen it, and worn the T-shirt, you just might. Why not keep an open mind and judge each step as you reach it? It's all up to you and you aren't committed until and unless you choose to be.

AA believe that alcoholism is a lifelong disease which, once contracted, can never be cured, though the symptoms can be abolished by taking the right measures. Because it is a disease, the person who has it is not at fault, so long as he does everything in his power to deal with it. This is the concept of 'illness behaviour' which applies across medicine. If you break your leg it is not your fault, but you must follow the advice given to you concerning bed rest, physiotherapy, etc. If you go for a run before your leg has healed, then you only have yourself to blame for the consequences.

AA, which is made up entirely of alcoholics, most 'in recovery' (abstinent from alcohol), has studied in detail the thinking problems and behaviour patterns that characterize alcoholism. The preamble[2] that starts most AA meetings explains the functions of AA much better than I can:

> Alcoholics Anonymous is a fellowship of men and women who share their experience, strength and hope with each other that they may solve their common problem and help others to recover from alcoholism. The only requirement for membership is a desire to stop drinking. There are no dues or fees for AA membership; we are self-supporting through our own contributions. AA is not allied with any sect, denomination, politics, organization or institution; does not wish to engage in any controversy; neither endorses nor opposes any causes. Our primary purpose is to stay sober and help other alcoholics to achieve sobriety.

AA then sets down 12 steps to recovery,[3] each one involving reading (there is a wealth of excellent AA literature to help), discussion and introspection in its achievement. Members are encouraged to work through these steps in order:

1 We admitted we were powerless over alcohol – that our lives had become unmanageable.
2 Came to believe that a Power greater than ourselves could restore us to sanity.
3 Made a decision to turn our will and our lives over to the care of God *as we understood Him.*
4 Made a searching and fearless moral inventory of ourselves.
5 Admitted to God, to ourselves and to another human being the exact nature of our wrongs.
6 Were entirely ready to have God remove all these defects of character.
7 Humbly asked Him to remove our shortcomings.

---

[2] 'Copyright © by The AA Grapevine, Inc.; reprinted with permission.

[3] The Twelve Steps are reprinted with permission of Alcoholics Anonymous World Services, Inc. Permission to reprint the Twelve Steps does not mean that AA has reviewed or approved the contents of this publication, nor that AA agrees with the views expressed herein. AA is a program of recovery from alcoholism *only* – use of the Twelve Steps in connection with programs and activities which are patterned after AA, but which address other problems, or in any other non-AA context, does not imply otherwise.

8 Made a list of all persons we had harmed, and became willing to make amends to them all.
9 Made direct amends to such people wherever possible, except when to do so would injure them or others.
10 Continued to take personal inventory and when we were wrong promptly admitted it.
11 Sought through prayer and meditation to improve our conscious contact with God, *as we understood Him*, praying only for knowledge of His will for us and the power to carry that out.
12 Having had a spiritual awakening as a result of these steps, we tried to carry this message to alcoholics, and to practise these principles in all our affairs.

These steps are suggestions, not rules. They are flexible and broad; no one will tell you exactly how you must interpret them. Indeed, AA's *big book* states 'The only requirement for membership is a desire to give up drinking.' Nobody is going to force you to follow the steps, and many, in the early days of sobriety, just go to AA meetings to listen. What is agreed by most people who succeed in staying sober with AA is that working on the steps in *some* way is essential for a continuing and happy recovery. I won't go through the steps in detail here as they are beyond the scope of this book, but I will say that I think the first step is the hardest. Admitting your alcoholism takes a lot of courage.

The tendency to minimize and deny one's problem is very strong in many people with drink problems. The most extreme example of this that I have witnessed was the patient who catalogued the changes in his life since he had started to drink heavily. He told me he had lost his wife and family, his job, his house and his driving licence, he had a stomach ulcer, had started having epileptic seizures and, shortly before I saw him, had nearly died of liver failure. When I referred to his drink problem he protested, 'I haven't got a drink problem, I could give it up any time I like.' This man will never turn his life around and start the climb back to health and happiness until he accepts that he suffers from alcoholism. There is nothing that I or anyone else can do to make him decide this, because the harder one tries the stronger will he resist and deny, until he is ready. One hopes that his 'rock bottom', the point at which he has gone so low that he decides to change, will come soon because he hasn't got much time. This is an extreme example, but a degree of denial is almost universal in people with drink problems.

Other examples from my recent experience include the chap who arrived at a session intoxicated. 'It isn't my fault,' he protested. 'I had to have whisky in my coffee this morning because the milk had gone off.' Or the fellow who registered nearly twice the legal driving limit on the alcometer. 'Well,' he mused, 'all I can think is that it must have been the *coq au vin* I had for supper last night.'

This symptom of alcoholism is a bar to any progress and must be overcome before you can get anywhere. Taking an honest look at yourself and your drinking, with the help of AA, is the biggest step towards recovery.

Most useful of all is the support provided by AA through their weekly meetings and provision of a 'sponsor' – a fellow alcoholic in recovery who will act as your own personal support and safety valve. You can phone your sponsor whenever you need to, particularly if you feel at risk of having a drink. AA is quite clear that an alcoholic can never control his drinking. 'One drink is too many and ten are not enough.'

They suggest that you go to a lot of meetings at first as you need a lot of support. Some recommend 90 meetings in 90 days, others three a week for the first year or two. Attendance is a lifelong commitment (though at a lesser frequency later). Most don't find it a chore, but a joy and a highlight of their lives.

There is a lot of conjecture in the medical world as to whether or not alcoholism is a disease, but while the academics argue this one out, AA most often will help you do something about it. A visit commits you to nothing and is well worth a try. What have you got to lose? For more information, contact The AA General Service Office, PO Box 1, Stonebow House, York YOI 2NJ or visit www.alcoholics-anonymous. org.uk.

If you want to know more, I suggest you read *Living Sober* (Alcoholics Anonymous World Services Inc., 1975, printed in Great Britain by Hazell, Watson & Viney Ltd, Aylesbury, Bucks).

What follows is a short account of one AA member's experiences, which may help to illustrate how AA can help. You may recognize some of her patterns of behaviour. If so, the conclusion, I hope, is obvious. Her name has been changed for the purpose of anonymity. This, as its name suggests, is a very important principle of AA, so your secrets are safe. I am immensely grateful to her for sharing her story with me and with you.

Anne's story

This is the true story of a person who, together with many others, has come to know the value of AA.

Anne's drinking had been increasing for years; she was deeply ashamed of this, but managed to deny her problem to herself and others. Her life was descending into chaos. When her partner eventually threatened to leave her if she didn't stop drinking, she stopped. She congratulated herself for having overcome drinking in her own way, and felt that her achievement showed how in control she was.

What Anne didn't realize at the time – or at least if she did, she didn't admit it to herself – was that she was still dependent. She wasn't drinking, but she was still behaving and thinking like an addict. She was shoplifting, she had become increasingly promiscuous; she was taking tranquillizers when the guilt got too much, and all the while she was becoming more and more dependent on her partner. The more pills she took, the worse became her bouts of depression. At times she felt so bitter, angry and sorry for herself that she considered suicide. Her life was purposeless and painful. Now, looking back on this time, she says: 'I was dependent on anything and anyone. I told myself that I would be OK as long as my partner stayed with me. But it was inevitable that I would drink; it was just a matter of time.'

Sure enough, as soon as her relationship broke down she started drinking again, blaming her partner for her relapse. This time, her drinking escalated more rapidly than before and as it did so, her life fell apart with alarming speed. She started to drink at work, and was soon disciplined for this. She drove while under the influence. She developed ways of hiding her drinking from colleagues, friends, family – and even from herself; she bought wine boxes so that she couldn't see the speed at which the level was falling; she would hide a bottle in her handbag and drink it in the toilet with the tap running so that no one could hear her drinking. Countless times she would arrange to meet people and then forget that these arrangements had been made. Large chunks of her life became blanks as she found herself more and more frequently drunk. Gradually her friends and family started drifting away. With her problems mounting, drink seemed to be the only way she could temporarily forget them.

Eventually she decided to go to her GP. She braced herself to tell him everything. She now sees this as the day that her life turned around; the day she started on the road to real recovery.

Fortunately for Anne, her GP had a contact in AA called Pat, who he knew had been in recovery for some time, was working on the twelve steps, and would be happy to talk to anyone who wanted help. Pat phoned her and they met. They got on well and Anne agreed to go to an AA meeting with her. As it turned out, she went to several different meetings and Pat became her sponsor. As sponsor, Pat acted as friend, guide, confidante and stimulus to action – but she was careful to ensure that Anne developed a network of friends in AA so she didn't become dependent on her alone.

Anne was so used to hiding her feelings, or covering them up by drinking, that at first she found the openness and emotion that she encountered in some of the meetings alarming. For the first four months that she was there, she didn't speak at all. That was OK; nobody had to speak in a meeting unless they wanted to. But she listened, and slowly her scepticism was overcome as she heard other people's stories and recognized similarities with her own. Initially, she tried to rationalize this by telling herself 'they are much worse than me' – but the more meetings she attended, the less she needed or wanted to take this way out. Eventually she started to talk, and the week before her first 'birthday' in AA, she shared her full story. She was horribly nervous to begin with, but the support she received helped her to overcome her fears.

This, then, was the starting point, and Anne's life has since turned around. She has now been in six years of recovery, and is a very happy and independent person. She went to four meetings a week to begin with, but now goes to a couple per week – these are still a central part of her life; they always will be.

I will share here a few insights that Anne, through her experiences in AA, has shared with me.

She is saddened that some people reject AA because of the references to a 'higher power'. She is clear that a search for spirituality is important, but not necessarily straightaway: 'I can't see the problem,' she says. 'Once you get involved, life changes so much that you can't escape the conclusion that something bigger than you is at work. Nobody will have to persuade you; you'll do that for yourself in time.'

She and other AA members find it important to take life one day at a time: 'Don't worry about what might happen next week. By all means make plans about what you are going to do, but don't plan the outcome. This doesn't mean that you can sit back; if you are going to stay sober, you have to change. After all, if nothing changes, you'll stay the same.'

She points out that action works – worry doesn't: 'Try worrying as hard as you can for five minutes, then work out what has changed. Is it worth it?'

Anne has been working on all the steps of recovery for some years now and doesn't intend to stop. She feels she is putting back some of what she has taken from AA and, in doing so, she says that she has lost the self-centredness that characterized her addiction. She remembers, when drinking, saying to herself, 'There must be more to life than this.' There was.

Now Anne is facing reality rather than railing against it and suppressing her feelings. 'With every year of sobriety, life gets better, because I get better. I knew I was getting better when I could look out of the window in the morning and let it rain. I don't want everything my way all the time now.'

I hope Anne's story will encourage more people to make contact with AA.

A few of my favourite sayings from AA members

You may think of people who go to AA as a miserable lot who just recount their woes. In fact, the opposite is true. I find them challenging, sometimes funny, risqué, but rarely dull. I like the way some have of using humour to illustrate alcoholic thinking. Here are a few of their *bons mots*:

Man take drink
Drunk take drink
Then, drink take man!
(They say this comes from Confucius).

Denial is not a river in Egypt.

A man falls over a cliff.
As he falls, he grabs hold of the only
Bush growing over the cliff edge.

'If there's anybody up there, help me,' he shouts.

The clouds part and a ray of light hits him.
A voice booms out.
'Let go, my son and I will help you.'

The man thinks for a moment, then shouts back,
'Is there anybody else up there?'

(What have you got which will do better than AA?)

Part 5
IF YOU HAVEN'T RUN INTO PROBLEMS YET

11

Sensible drinking

As I have mentioned before, sensible drinking is not an option for most people who have had a serious drink problem. Life is just as good without booze; but if you and everyone around you agree that you have never had a problem, then the thing is to ensure that you never develop one. This means, if you drink, drinking sensibly. Try the drink diary mentioned in Chapter 9 to check on your consumption.

There is only one valid reason for drinking alcohol, and that is for recreation. Don't use it for any other purpose and never have a drink because you need one. Various points are obvious. It is unwise to drink and drive, to drink every day, to drink during the working day, and to exceed the recommended weekly consumption of units. Don't binge-drink (drinking to get drunk). It is no longer unfashionable to have a soft drink at a party or gathering; all considerate hosts provide a selection of soft drinks. At work lunches, too, it is the norm these days to have something like sparkling water or even tap water, rather than an alcoholic drink.

In my opinion (and this is a personal one) the essence of sensible drinking is to treat it as an art form. You don't go to the theatre or cinema every day; to do so would be to devalue it, and you don't judge the merit of a film by its length. Equally, drinking every day makes it less enjoyable, and the best drinks are not the strongest.

I have never known a dependent drinker who takes care over the preparation of a drink. He is only concerned to get a high blood alcohol level as quickly as possible. Of course, it is possible for a jetsetter to develop a drink problem exclusively from champagne, but in my experience he doesn't select it with any interest and treats it with contempt, pouring it down the hatch without ceremony. I think that a sensible drinker is a civilized drinker. Clean and attractive glasses, a slice of lemon in the gin and tonic, the imaginative and well-presented cocktail, using good mixers rather than cheap or home-made versions, hunting for a pub that keeps a really good beer, and attending to the bouquet of a wine are to me hallmarks of a person who treats a drink properly rather than as a means of lowering consciousness.

I would suggest avoiding certain drinks altogether. 'Special' beers and lagers (over 5 per cent alcohol) taste revolting to me and are often used to get drunk quickly. Barley wines are also often abused, though I have met a few sensible-drinking devotees. Vintage cider is mostly very high in alcohol and it is doubtful whether it is any more pleasant than weaker varieties. Cheap plonk is now very easily available, but I have never met anyone who says it tastes nice. This is only a personal view, and I know that some people drink these beverages sensibly. It comes back to my earlier point. If you drink occasionally for the enjoyment of the drink and not to get drunk, you shouldn't run into problems.

Of course, most of us are not millionaires and can't afford *premier cru* claret every week. I have an admission to make here. I am a fan of good wines and I can tell you that nowadays it isn't an expensive hobby if indulged in occasionally and if the wine is selected carefully. Australian, Bulgarian and Spanish wines can be excellent and very inexpensive. I have found Hugh Johnson's *Pocket Wine Book* and everything by Robert Parker very useful and great money-savers.

I am not suggesting that wine-tasting or drinking any other alcoholic beverage should be your main recreation; there is much more to life than booze, but if you have never had a drink problem, sensible drinking can be safe and enjoyable.

Be merry, not drunk.

Index